"In Dr. William Hutch_____ *age Maximized*, he theorizes _____ marriage to be a selfless, sacrificial love to weld a couple into one. He masterfully weaves a literary perspective with a spiritual viewpoint for couples to not lose sight of God, the divine purpose for marriage, the divine love necessary to fulfill that purpose, and the expression of that love through lowering one's self under our partner to lift him or her up to God. One of Dr. Hutcheson's myriad talents is writing in a conversational tone – reading his book is like having a meaningful conversation with a dear friend. His use of personality types/styles to bridge the communication gap (which we experience in all of our relationships) arms us with the tools with which we can improve and offer our significant others fidelity, trust, and openness. *Marriage Maximized* has given me a greater understanding of the inherent needs of men and women and I feel as if I have been offered an opportunity to maximize the happiness in my life *and* my marriage. What a gift this book is!"

– Heidi Hulsey Fowler, *Mother & Entrepreneur*

Marriage Maximized should be required reading for everyone who desires to be married someday and for all of us who already are.

William Hutcheson is an expert guide for this wonderful journey of marriage, presenting profound truths in a simple manner and sharing with us important insights, not only about marriage itself, but about our partner and, very importantly, ourselves.

Reading this book, I was reminded of basic principles for a great relationship and, even after over forty-seven years of marriage, learned exciting new ways to express to my wife my deep love and commitment to her. As a result, I know the best is yet to be.

This book will guide the reader in the steps necessary to become a better person and to have a marriage that is forever filled with purpose and passion/fun and fulfillment."

– Alan Smith, *Th.d., Pastor, Church at Decatur Heights, Decatur, GA*

"This book was very comforting to me in several ways. From almost the first page, I felt like Bill was inside my marriage. I felt understood and less alone. And he gave me hope that change is possible. Life can be the way it once was – happiness wasn't just the fairy tale of a young bride. We can find it again. There is hope."

– Betsy Chaput, *Entrepreneur in Communications*

"Most of us would probably agree when contemplating something as serious as marriage that advice and counsel from a trusted source is invaluable. As a Christian, advice and mentoring from a pastor who has a Christ-centered and influenced message is essential for a happy and successful marriage.

Marriage Maximized by William Hutcheson is a book that I believe can help every marriage, whether a couple is contemplating marriage or has been married and wants to make the relationship better. The author's gift to mentor and shepherd people from a practical and Christ-centered perspective makes *Marriage Maximized* a valuable resource for all marriages.

It's been a privilege of mine to know the author for almost fifty years, and his faith and walk with Christ have served as a personal inspiration to me and many others that know him. He is one of the people I look at as proof God still raises up people in this age to lead people in the Christian faith in uncertain times. *Marriage Maximized* is a reflection if this walk, and his offering to help everyone's marriage."

– James B. Cavendish, *R.P.A./M.S*

"Just start reading the first few pages and you will be hooked! With years of helping couples and families navigate the rough terrain of life, Bill knows what he's talking about. Based on solid Biblical principles, *Marriage Maximized* offers practical solutions to help marriages at any stage of life. This is not a book you read and put away. You will find yourself highlighting and rereading as you sense the power of the Holy Spirit at work in your heart. What a privilege to have his years of anointed ministry experience put into a volume from which many will benefit!"

– Della Lago, *Church Administrator*

"My biggest takeaway from reading the book is a sense of renewed encouragement. As a middle-aged woman who has been happily married for nearly twenty-five years, but who has also dedicated much time and energy to mothering five children and weathering the normal storms of life, I can identify with feeling like the marriage has settled into a place that needs new life and renewal breathed into it.

I believe that for the most part our marriage has always been on Charity Lane. I love this metaphor. So for me it is not so much about taking a detour off of Happiness Boulevard and onto Charity Lane, but more about doing some critical road repair and maintenance to remind ourselves that Charity Lane is indeed the best path to realize the Divine intimacy that God designed for our marriage.

The book lays out practical, meaningful, and attainable goals to help marriages either get on the right path or recommit to following the right path and staying the course."

– Joy Coe, *freelance writer and editor, middle school Latin teacher, and Christ follower*

Marriage Maximized

marriage maximized

The Guide to a Purposeful and Passionate Relationship

WILLIAM
HUTCHESON

NEW YORK

LONDON • NASHVILLE • MELBOURNE • VANCOUVER

marriage maximized

The Guide to a Purposeful and Passionate Relationship

Published in New York, New York, by Morgan James Publishing in partnership with Difference Press Morgan James is a trademark of Morgan James, LLC.
www.MorganJamesPublishing.com

ISBN 9781642796360 paperback
ISBN 9781642796377 eBook
ISBN 9781642796384 audiobook
Library of Congress Control Number: 2019943452

Cover Design by:
Rachel Lopez
www.r2cdesign.com

Interior Design by:
Chris Treccani
www.3dogcreative.net

Morgan James is a proud partner of Habitat for Humanity Peninsula and Greater Williamsburg. Partners in building since 2006.

Get involved today! Visit
MorganJamesPublishing.com/giving-back

For Mary Beth – my life-time bride, companion, confidant, and best friend, who remained committed, loyal, forgiving and patient as I learned how to be a cherishing husband.

TABLE OF CONTENTS

CHAPTER 1

"Will We Ever Again Know Happiness?"

Hi! An important search led you here. You may have searched for a while.

Your quest may have begun today. You no longer can ignore 'it,' because 'it' is missing in your marriage – and has been for some time now. You want 'it' back! You long for, pray for, and look for the happiness that went AWOL.

You remember it, right? Remember how you felt in those early dating days? You knew this relationship was the one! That first meeting, or that first date, wow! The chemistry was undeniable. You shared so much in common. The hours you spent together collapsed into what felt like minutes. You couldn't believe how quickly they passed. You felt so special in his presence.

The next day you thought about that date with every unoccupied mind-moment. You replayed the conversation, you remembered his strong, handsome features. The magic of that evening lingered for days and gave you such hope for the second date.

When that time neared, you could hardly wait to see him again. The conversation flowed just as easily. You swear your hands sparked when he reached out to take your hand. You swelled with pride as you two walked together. Again, the clock traveled too quickly. The evening ended with firecrackers exploding in your chest when you kissed. You called this state of euphoria "happiness." It possessed you. Wave after wave rolled over you.

What about the day the two of you finally pulled the engagement trigger? You felt the tsunami of happiness wash over you. The proposal, the ring, the setting – all perfect! You may, or may not, have expected the proposal, but when he popped the question, you accepted through tears of joy! That day charged you two with enough happy energy to carry you through all the planning. When the details became overwhelming, or some part of the plan didn't work out as you had hoped, you looked back to the proposal and remembered how happy you felt. That joyous moment still welled up in your eyes and ran down your cheeks. Your happiness meter pegged out again and you soldiered on to your goal!

After all of your planning, you finally reached the wedding day. Enough of the dream materialized to set the stage for the day of a lifetime. The dress – you couldn't wait to be seen in that dress! The flowers beautifully framed the place he waited. The music set the romantic atmosphere. Then you saw his face – he beamed as you walked toward him. There you were, surrounded by family and friends, saying the vows and exchanging the rings. Blissful reality! How could such an important moment, such a happy moment, happen so quickly? How could a lifetime be launched in a matter of minutes?

Even as those thoughts faded and your attention returned, you heard the pastor pronounce that by the authority of God and the state, you were married! Yes, married!! Your new life together began with a kiss. While still embraced, you heard for the first time, "May I be the first to present to you Mr. and Mrs..." and the music sent you two off into a wonderful, happy life together.

And the honeymoon! You'd never felt happier than by his side or in his arms those memorable few days! Pixie dust must have been sprinkled on those days. You walked around in a storybook setting. You laughed. You drank in each other's life like parched ground in a summer rain. The colors seemed brighter. The smells sweeter. The meals all seemed five-star because you were together as wife and husband. You strolled beneath the brightest stars and seemed robed in the soft moonlight. Each day proved memorable, but the nights were magical. How could you be happier?

Post-honeymoon days continued the happy theme. Folding two lives into one presented challenges, but you met each one with happy resolve before which the challenge melted. You returned to work, but enjoyed the spontaneity of last-minute rendezvous for dinner, dropping the laundry duty for a trip to the movie theater, or immediately answering that "come hither" glance. Routine returned, days turned into months, and months passed into a year or two. You accepted routine but wanted to keep the happiness.

Did you begin to notice the changes when your little blessing arrived, or when the great work promotion added stress that drained much of life's sweet spontaneity? You found yourselves needing to plan your fun or relaxation days or even weeks in advance. Impulsive intimacy became rare. You loved each other no less, but you thought frequently about those carefree, happy days of dating and together setting up your home.

And somewhere along life's way you make another job move, move into a larger home with a larger mortgage, or receive the blessing of a couple more children, who don't just knock, but kick at adolescence's door. Your family, your home, and your careers may parallel your dreams for life. There's just this one thing. Your marriage appears fine to everyone else. You've settled into a comfortable life together. The bills get paid. You take care of the family together. You enjoy friends. Together you plan the annual family vacation and enjoy it. You survey your situation and feel blessed. *Yet*, you miss the happiness and with it the passion and excitement you once experienced. And you want it back!

You are not alone! Many couples quietly harbor the very same concern. You wonder what's wrong... why don't we feel as happy as before? You may have asked, "Am I at fault? Have I lost something that changed our relationship? Do those few extra pounds or my weekends without makeup or my 'casual' wardrobe rob our relationship of its happiness?"

Perhaps you've wondered if he's lost interest. Does the stress of the job distract him so much that your happiness suffers? After all, sometimes when he's home his mind is still at work. Once or twice questions about his fidelity snuck into your thoughts like a roach crawling out of the darkness. You quickly squashed that filthy notion. He loves you, but the notice of something missing finally morphed into fear.

Fear spawned other ugly thoughts in the form of the dreaded "what ifs." In your unguarded moments, they attacked. "What if he's quietly unhappy?" Later, "What if his eyes start wandering as he looks for happiness?" Even worse, "What if he wants a divorce?"

What would that do to your kids? They would be devastated. They had rarely heard you argue. How would they take divorce? The thought of hurting them nearly loosens your now-tenuous grip on your emotions.

How could you face your parents? You told them he was the one. You announced that this marriage was for life. Would they be disappointed in you? Memories of childhood hijinks and teenaged antics that creased their brows with disappointment still haunt you. How deeply disappointed divorce would make them! Intolerable!

You would be disappointed in you. In fact, you sniff the rancid odor of failure just thinking about divorce. Apart from a few uncharacteristic missteps, your path remained straight and narrow. If your marriage veered, it was gradual and unintentional. No, sir, you made no sharp turns to the right or left. What a tragedy for a gradual, unintended fading of happiness to undo the "I do." To push the marriage off course would be disappointing, but to allow it to drift off course into divorce seems worse.

And how could you face the future alone? The mere thought of doing life alone pulled a knot in your stomach. Even though you generally feel confident in yourself, you don't want to face life alone – without him. You two decided to face life together. Oh, not alone!

The last fear grew largest: How could you face God after you said an "I do" that meant you would for a lifetime? With that thought, guilt growled at your door. What had you done to lose a happy marriage? What had you failed to do to make the marriage happy? God had been so good to bring you into this relationship. You couldn't allow it to fail. You don't want to fail God. You don't want to fail your mate. You don't want to fail your children. You don't want to fail your family. So, you beg, "Oh, God, help me! Help us!"

Okay, you wake from the day-mare of your worst fears. Don't we humans always seem to rush first toward the worst conclusions? At first, you fantasize about snapping your fingers and magically having happiness return. Then life would be great! Yet, no one sells a Marital Book of Magical Incantations. You find no lamp to rub and no genie to grant your wishes. You turn from fantasy and entertain practical ends.

Something must be done before any of those "what ifs" turned to reality! Maybe a change of scenery may do the trick. What about a romantic weekend away, time for some overdue passion, a good dose of laughter, and a few slow walks hand-in-hand through a garden? What if you could return to the site of your honeymoon? Stay in the same room! Walk on the same beach in the evening and dine under the same stars at night.

Reality quickly bursts that bubble. Even if the bank account could tolerate such a luxury, the kids' weekend activities and childcare would put that dream out of reach. Yet, you're convinced you must do something. You've invested so much already in the marriage. You've poured money and time into the family. What value exactly would you put on your marriage after the precious life invested in it?

Faced with hard financial realities that prevent any extravagance, another line of thinking may enter. If you've searched for a while, or if you've tried to recapture the feeling with an event but have been unsuccessful, you may be wondering if this is all you will have. You may wonder if other people at work or in the neighborhood or at church cover their wants and fears with smiling faces. You may not hold dear enough a friend to confess your wants and fears. That level of transparency scares you! What else may they see? What else may you see within?!

"Well," you may think, "just accept the status quo and be grateful for what you do have. Life isn't so bad. Our marriage could be much worse. Maybe I held too high a standard and dreamed for too much. Maybe this is as good as anyone should expect."

Something within steers you away from settling for the status quo. To settle, to attempt no improvement, to embrace mediocrity sits on your spirit like a light case of nausea. It's more than uncomfortable but less than sickening. You at least take a couple of antacids in the case of a queasy stomach. You're not willing to live with a queasy spirit without taking something!

After all, you know you still love him. You think he still loves you. You both love the children. Your marriage compares very well to most couples you know. It's just not as good as it could be – as it used to be. You want a return to the happiness you remember. So, you search and you hope.

Well, don't give up now. You may be closer than you realize to answering your question, "Will I ever again know happiness in this marriage?" You've come this far. What follows in this book will give you a new, or at least a renewed, perspective on marriage that promises to lead you to a better marriage than you thought possible. Then I offer some very practical, doable, and effective tools for you together to build even more than a happy marriage— tools to *maximize your marriage*.

CHAPTER 2:

How Can I Help You Find Happiness and Maximize Marriage?

The short answer to that question looks like this: thirty-eight years of developing a unique process for improving marriages, refined by working with between 200 and 300 couples. Even more important is my own journey and marriage.

My Journey

As a mid-teen, I sensed an inner unsettling. I've since come to recognizing those feelings as nudges from God.

I struggled for clarification of God's nudges, but to no avail. My family and pastor could not interpret them for me. After a year or so, the nudges faded. I wrongly assumed God had finished whatever nudging He would do, or maybe I experienced spiritual indigestion. I moved on from high school to college.

I discovered the Psychology Department at Mercer University (Macon, GA) during my freshman year. My life's direction was settled: "I'll be a counselor!" The first course hooked me. A desire to help others already existed. This education promised to give it a skeleton and skin.

I initially dreamt of being a psychiatrist, at least until I interviewed one who described the educational journey required. I couldn't stomach med school – literally! I felt faint at the sight of physical trauma and blood. How would I make it through anatomy and physiology, much less hospital rounds? I didn't realize as a college freshman that a psychiatrist is an M.D.

Undaunted, I veered toward clinical psychology. No med school lay before such a therapist. However, in my sophomore year, winter quarter, God nudged me in a different direction.

In February 1974, just when I thought my next five years were set, God renewed the nudgings. What exactly did I experience? My mind felt distracted. I found concentration on any task difficult. My appetite increased (I'm a comfort eater). Satisfaction in what I generally found interesting and fun faded. At some point in the month I realized God was stirring my pot.

First, I liked the direction before me and didn't want any changes. Second, I feared that God would call me to the pastorate, and I did not want to be a pastor. How could a bearded, longish-haired, bell-bottom wearing, semi-rebellious kid fit into the role of a pastor? I respected the men who pastored our congregation. They possessed sterling characters and served well, but they slicked back their wavy locks and generally wore small, round-rimmed glasses and three-piece suits. I didn't fit that mold. I dressed casually, even on Easter Sunday. I enjoyed southern rock music, especially our hometown Allman Brothers Band. My glasses rims were trendy. And inwardly, I didn't feel worthy.

God's uncomfortable nudgings threatened my plans. They were rather unwelcome.

After weeks of intense debate with God, I surrendered – or at least compromised, "Okay, Lord, I'll be a Christian counselor!" I finished Mercer University with a B.A. in Christianity and enrolled in 1976 as a theology student at the Southern Baptist Theological Seminary in Louisville, KY. There I planned to spend all of my elective hours in the Pastoral Care/Counseling department, where I would work on a degree to become a clinical counselor. The way seemed reasonable and set.

God has a sense of humor!

The nudging began again in the winter of '78. This time the pot-stirrer God used was Dr. Edward Byrd. I had taken his one-hour course on the *Life and Work of the Pastor*. I took the class only to get an A. God had other plans!

After a couple of weeks I began to sense something like a magnet drawing me toward the pastorate. I rationalized that it was nothing more than Dr. Byrd's winsome personality. The drawing grew stronger. It occupied those moments when my mind wasn't focused on studying. I couldn't be a pastor. I wasn't cut out of a pastoral bolt of cloth. As a believer, I felt my pattern cut on the bias, often against the grain of the Church. Yet, the more I rationalized the stronger the attraction grew. I had to face the fear!

This time the nudges clearly pushed me toward the pastorate. After a much shorter, less intense debate, I surrendered to God's direction. I shifted my study focus toward the pastorate. Upon graduation in 1980, my wife, Mary Beth, and I headed to southern Georgia for my first pastorate.

God doesn't waste anything. I carried into pastoral ministry several assets: a desire to help individuals, a bent toward pastoral counseling, a God-given ability to read people and relate to them well, and a gift for teaching. By applying those tools to the early opportunities presented, God parlayed the combination into a process for helping couples – those nearly-wed, to better prepare for marriage, and established couples, to improve their marriages.

While the dream of becoming a clinical counselor never materialized, God wove those different threads of desire into a pastoral process to improve relationships. Now, in retirement, I am blessed to combine the three things I enjoyed most in my pastoral career into a marriage coaching ministry: teaching, helping couples, and mentoring in the spiritual life.

The Process Developed

Here's what motivated the development of the process I use today. Two months or so before our January '78 wedding, my bride-to-be and I met with her pastor. Brother Troy arranged for us to meet in his church study for a "conference." We had no idea what subjects he'd bring up. My honey, Mary Beth, feared the venerable old pastor would discuss sex! He didn't. We discussed love for ten minutes. We discussed the dates and places and times for rehearsal and ceremony. We discussed the division of service since another of Mary Beth's pastors would participate. We finished thirty minutes later with a prayer. After our conference, we were no better prepared for what lay ahead.

Early into my first pastorate a young couple presented me with my first opportunity as pastor to conduct a wedding. I agreed. We discussed rehearsal and ceremony dates and places. The conversation limply ended. I wasn't sure what to do next. One thing I knew, however, I would offer them more than my wife and I were offered by way of marriage preparation.

With a desire to provide better pre-marriage preparation, and without having been taught a process for helping couples prepare for marriage, I began creating a process that first consisted of communication training. The ability to communicate well gives marriage a fighting chance, especially when a couple experiences conflict. So, I laid the cornerstone of my coaching process with a session with exercises that lasted 60 to 90 minutes.

A couple of years after coaching this first couple, I discovered an inventory that expanded my coaching preparation. Feedback suggested that two or so hours of preparation proved helpful. So, I became more proficient in explaining and using the inventory. Phase two of development lasted four or five years. Then I learned of a relatively new inventory, developed by a counselor and with the input of many counselors. The PREPARE Inventory measured couple agreement on ten different issues that counselors found build the strongest marriages. The PREPARE Inventory sits atop my process as the keystone that holds the process part together.

In 1991 I began my doctoral work. In the first seminar, we twelve students took the Myers-Briggs Type Indicator (MBTI). While I had heard of the MBTI, I had never taken the test. When the results returned and were interpreted later that week, my jaw dropped when I realized how accurately it identified me! Immediately I knew this would prove very helpful for the couples I would coach.

I brought a version of the MBTI, called the Kiersey Temperament Sorter (KTS), home from the seminar. Mary Beth became my first guinea pig. I explained what the MBTI/KTS revealed about my personality. She nodded in agreement. We identified her personality. Voila! We discovered that I am a strong extravert and that she is just as strong an introvert. As we discussed the implication an amazing insight arose. We realized why our tiffs often became more intense. As an introvert, my bride needed time to go inside her mind and think through her responses before she spoke. As an extravert, I needed to "think out loud." So, in our first home, the kitchen connected to the dining room, which opened to the living room, that led to the hall and front door, and the hall also connected with the kitchen. Why is that important? Well, many of our tiffs started in the kitchen. Mary Beth would back into the dining room and I'd follow. Then she'd turn to the living room and sit down. I'd follow, arguing each step. Then she'd get up and return through the hall to the kitchen. Guess what? I followed.

Extraverted Bill needed to "talk out" the issue. Introverted Mary Beth needed time to gather her thoughts, then talk. I saw her backing away as a refusal to deal with the issue. She saw my following as pushing her, almost as bullying!

Once we saw this dance as a function of our differing personalities, we chose to honor our differences. I honored her introversion by saying, "Okay, how long do you think you will need to think about this?" She'd reply with thirty minutes, or an hour. We agreed to meet back together in the allotted time. If she needed more time, I'd back away. I was in trouble if she said, "I don't know! I'll find you!" This one discovery about our differing personalities changed our conflict patterns to shorter, less discordant disagreements. That translated to fewer apologies needed on my part!

The last cog in the process workings appeared in the mid-90's, when I discovered a bestselling book, *The Five Love Languages*, written by Christian counselor Dr. Gary

Chapman. Immediately upon reading his book, I saw the very practical application of the kind of love God means to characterize marriage. Again, Mary Beth and I became my first test case. We gained an understanding of the five love languages, took the test, and realized some very helpful points about our different primary love languages. I will explain these languages in more detail later in the book, but for now, I'll say that Mary Beth's primary love language is Quality Time (QT). Mine is Physical Touch (PT). Our difference came into poignant clarity for me one evening. Mary Beth greeted me at the door when I arrived home. I gave her a good kiss, slapped her on the bottom, and disappeared to change clothes for dinner. Mary Beth has always been faithful to greet family members and see them off. Her hugs and kisses energized me.

After dinner, I suggested that she sit in the den as I washed the dinner dishes. With the task completed and with a deep sense of "well-done Bill," I rounded the corner into the den, expecting to see a note of gratitude in Mary Beth's face. After all, I washed the dishes, cleaned the stove and table, and allowed her a few minutes of well-deserved rest. Instead of gratitude, I saw anger in her eyes. I jumped on the defense in my mind, "How could she be upset! I just washed the dishes, VOLUNTARILY!" A brief and contentious exchange ensued. Thankfully, she came quickly to the point and I heard it: "I'd rather you do the dishes *with* me than to do the dishes *for* me!" A 150-watt bulb scattered the darkness of my self-satisfied pride and ignorance of my wife's needs. She needed to be with me

– classic QT. I offered her that day a love expressed as Physical Touch, kiss and bottom pop, and Acts of Service, washing dishes and cleaning the kitchen. She appreciated those expressions, but they didn't "speak" her primary love language.

Now, each day I know Mary Beth needs at least fifteen minutes of knee-to-knee time when she arrives home from her voice studio at the local university. If she's had a particularly trying day, she may need thirty to forty-five minutes of QT. When given, she feels valued, appreciated, loved. And it's a good thing for our marriage.

The process took shape over the first ten to fifteen years of pastoring. My first 100+ couples helped to shape the process. New tools added along the way the next decade brought the form to maturity. Another 150+ couples in that decade and the next helped to tweak and refine the process.

God chose this would-be counselor, initially-reluctant pastor to love and serve three congregations for thirty-six years. Now, in my retirement from congregational ministry, I combine three of my greatest passions: helping couples with a unique process, teaching, and mentoring couples and individuals in the spiritual life.

Not Coincidental

One final word before concluding: I don't believe you picked up this book by accident. I believe your interest reflects divine appointment. My faith in a benevolent and sovereign God allows no room for coincidence, chance, or blind fate. Instead, my worldview captures the picture of God gently guiding you to this book. You had the choice to respond or not. You picked up the book. Something caught your initial interest. May I really stretch that benevolent sovereignty point further? I believe God had you in mind when granting the inspiration to develop the process included here and for me to write this book.

What do I have to offer you? I offer you forty-two+ years of preparation – spiritual, emotional, educational, and experiential – poured into a unique process meant to help you find what you desire and more—what God desires for you. I offer you God's invitation to a marriage maximized.

CHAPTER 3:

Open to a Less-Traveled Way?

You desire what everyone seeks – an extraordinary marriage. Who can imagine anyone saying in subdued tones, "I just want a mediocre marriage, with no happiness and no passion. Give me an ordinary relationship." No! You want a fantastic marriage, filled with excitement and passion. You want extraordinary!

We all do. The numbers tell the story. According to the CDC's National Center for Health Statistics Fast Facts page, the US recorded 2,245,404 couples married in 2016. The American Psychological Association website states that in Western cultures at least ninety percent of people marry before age fifty.

And why do so many of us marry? A survey conducted by Pew Research, entitled "8 facts about love and marriage in America" (Feb. 13, 2018), listed the top three reasons to marry as: Love (88%); Life-long Commitment (81%); and Companionship (76%). Imagine a marriage characterized by a life-long companionship filled with love! Yes, you'll take a double helping, please.

Sadly, the statistics demonstrate a different reality. The same CDC information yields 827,261 divorces in 2016, and that does not include the divorces in six states (California, Georgia, Hawaii, Minnesota, and New Mexico)! Just taking the average of the forty-four reporting states and adding that average for the six non-reporting states, you have a number just above 940,000 divorces. That means in 2016 the US marked 4.2 marriages/minute and 1.8 divorces/minute. Something is amiss.

Those dismal statistics notwithstanding, we remain optimists. You and I still seek extraordinary marriages. As one "tying the knot" for a score of couples, I sought to help those marriages experience lasting love and companionship. Over the course of my thirty-eight-year pastoral career I developed a process for that purpose. So far, the success rate among those couples I can follow hits the target between seventy-five and eighty-five percent. I don't pretend to be the glue. As I confessed in the last chapter, God blessed me with the desire, the opportunity, and the tools to develop the process. My part involves helping them understand marriage as a particular path carved out by the One who established marriage. I seek to equip those couples for the journey together. I encourage the couples to follow God's path with God's help and to use the tools they possess to meet the challenges along the marriage path. The couples and God do the heavy lifting!

The Path Less Chosen

Working with nearly-weds and established couples for three decades gave me a deeper, practical appreciation for Robert Frost's poem, "The Road Not Taken."

Frost's poem provides a picture that may be helpful for us. Think about two different paths of marriage – two ways of approaching marriage, or two marriage paradigms. The wear on one shows that most travel that path. The other path doesn't seem too different at the divergence, but that less-traveled path leads to vistas unseen on the more traveled road.

The way more often traveled I call "Happiness Boulevard." At first, this road may seem more appealing. It seems to offer exactly what you want. The path is broader and maybe a bit more level as far as you can see. The lights shine brighter on Happiness Boulevard. Music echoing from down the path seems fun. Most of the people you know choose Happiness Boulevard. As they begin their trek arm-in-arm, they appear to be happy. And for the first several miles they are convinced they chose the right path.

By contrast, the process I developed points the couple to a "road less traveled by." The on-ramp for the less traveled way sends the couple in a different direction and offers a model for marriage many will consider new. Actually, the less-traveled road compares to using back roads instead of interstate highways to visit family.

For many years our family used interstates as often as possible. As those highways became crowded and more dangerous, we began traveling the two-lane road through small towns and rural areas of Georgia to visit family. The pace slowed, but we witnessed beauty not seen on the superhighways and we often took advantage of the small-town offerings, like sundaes, or boiled peanuts! You southerners understand about boiled peanuts!!

Let's name the less traveled road "Charity Lane." The name reflects the central focus of a very popular passage from the Bible used at Christian weddings, 1 Corinthians 13. You may remember that chapter 13 ends with the words: *So now faith, hope, and love abide, these three; but the greatest of these is love.* In this part of Paul's letter, he focused on a very special form of love. Scholars translating the 1611 King James Version of the Bible chose the word *charity* to translate the word for love used in 1 Corinthians 13. I will discuss in a later chapter the different words for love used by the Greek language. For now, just know that the word "charity" aptly describes the love God intended to characterize human marriage. I agree with the King James Version scholars. The word *charity* fits well the definition of God's love for us and our divine love for each other. It captures a compassion of heart that willingly offers what has not been earned and is not necessarily deserved. Charity grows from a choice to give, not from an affinity for the receiver. It describes a selfless love. On Charity Lane one often meets this selfless compassion. In contrast, here's what you're more likely to hear on Happiness Boulevard:

"I love him because he's always there for me!" or "She's always there for me!" Contrast that with the charity kind of love that God gives us for the trip down Charity Lane. The bride or wife who understands the road less traveled would more likely state, "I love him because I'm always there for him!" The groom's reception speech would reflect the same love, "I love her because I'm always there for her!" If you cannot quite yet wrap your mind around this charity love, you will by the end of the next chapter. You can see the 180° difference in these two loves. The weddings may look and feel very similar and each couple may be very happy on their wedding day, but the other-focused love of a maximized marriage will make "all the difference" on the journey. Charity Lane love possesses the values God intended for marriage that Happiness Boulevard love misses.

Contemporary culture departed from the divine intention for marriage communicated by our Creator. The intention for marriage expressed most often by contemporary couples may sound much like the fairytale story ending we heard as children, "and they lived happily ever after." Very rarely does anyone actually use those words, but the hope for a fairytale marriage leaks out in comments like, "She makes me so happy," and "He's everything I've been looking for!" The "selfward" direction of those comments often betrays an unrealistic, fairytale-like concept of marriage and points the couple toward Happiness Boulevard.

The less-traveled road begins by understanding the divine purpose of marriage. Within God's purpose, we will discover a different love from the love most often found on Happiness Boulevard. God's love will be found on Charity Lane, with its fewer curves and its two narrower lanes. The relationship God fosters in the couple on Charity Lane may be characterized as "otherward." It's self-forgetful. Just look at some of the synonyms for charity: compassion, kindness, mercy, sympathy. Each one denotes one person moving toward another person with a selfless attitude.

Herein lies the genius of Charity Lane. The path may feel steeper at first. The terrain may present more challenging steps to take, but the air smells pure and the vistas excel anything seen on Happiness Boulevard. To state this in clear, practical language, God's way offers the couple even more than the other way. Marriage done God's way proves more fulfilling and longer lasting. Just one statistical study to demonstrate the point. A 2000-2001 study of 24,671 couples in the US on the influence of spiritual beliefs and marriage found that the more a couple agreed on their spiritual life, the closer they felt and the more satisfaction they realized in marriage. Couple closeness and improved satisfaction in marriage – wouldn't these make you happier? Yes, and shared spiritual beliefs also dramatically positively influences other factors, including communication, conflict resolution, family/ friend relationships, financial management, and sexual relationship, to name five more critical areas!

My joy for the past three decades has been to point people toward God and to coach couples for a journey down Charity Lane. I believe, know by experience, and have seen statistics demonstrate that married couples choosing Charity Lane fare better than marriages traveling Happiness Boulevard. God granted me the high privilege of better preparing couples for the road less traveled.

Understand too that the preparation for beginning the Charity Lane journey also equips a couple for a mid-course correction. If already married, you likely began the marriage journey on Happiness Boulevard. You didn't see Charity Lane on the marriage map. Maybe you didn't know it existed. The good news now is it's not too late to switch paths! Yes, this process was developed with nearly-weds in mind; however, I realized that the principles and tools worked well for established couples who sought to improve their relationships. My wife and I gradually shifted our marriage from Happiness Boulevard to Charity Lane. To be transparent with you, when I first laid eyes on Mary Beth, she stood on the front row of the sixty+ Seminary Choir on the first chapel service of our first Seminary semester. The 1,400 seat Alumni Chapel filled to near capacity that day. I sat near the front because Baptists believe the real estate at the rear of a sanctuary is more valuable, meaning there's more room up front. The four rows of the newly formed Seminary Choir poured in from both sides of the choir loft – men first, bass and tenors, then altos, and finally sopranos. I spotted her immediately, the fourth from the left side. Her blondish-brown hair hung down her back to nearly her waist, her green eyes flashed, her lips gently curled into a small smile. I was hooked! Hormones took over! I heard nearly nothing sung or said that Wednesday. I resolved to meet her. I must know if she was single and if she was available. For the next week, I stalked the campus looking for that beautiful woman in the front row.

We met the following Saturday at a Labor Day picnic. She was single and available! Two other guys at that picnic spied her and told me they were going to ask her out. Thankfully, I called first, secured a date, and we were engaged by the end of October! I first fell in lust for my wife, then I fell in selfward love before we married in January 1978. Over the last forty+ years, we realized that God intended differently. By God's grace, our selfward love has been turning into an otherward love and we have taken an off-ramp from Happiness Boulevard onto Charity Lane. God offers hope to all couples willing to adopt the divine intention for marriage and follow God's lead.

Equipping for the Journey

The questions remain now, "How do you equip couples for Charity Lane?" and "How do couples take the off-ramp from Happiness Boulevard to Charity Lane?" Allow me to describe briefly the components of the equipping process I've used.

Laying the Foundation

Just as one may argue that a house's foundation determines the stability of the whole structure, so I argue that laying the right spiritual understanding of marriage determines the stability of the whole marriage. The four corners of the foundation will be laid with material from Genesis 1:26f, Genesis 2:25, Luke 9:23f, and Ephesians 5:21-33. The Bible contains much more about God's purpose and intention for marriage, but these passages set the foundation for understanding the purpose and realizing the intention.

Personalities

We will observe the two personalities that make up your marriage, both your similarities and differences. Some perceive these differences as a threat to relationship and happiness. Actually, when rightly appreciated as gifts from God, the difference will be received as strengths.

This chapter of the book will introduce you to the very basic concepts of this personality inventory called the Keirsey Temperament Sorter. You will also be directed to a website that offers a free test of your personality and gives you a thorough general explanation. If you react as most who take this inventory for the first time, you will be blown away by its accuracy.

The Love Languages

Identifying what "love language" your companion speaks may prove to be the first step toward the passion you seek! You will learn about the Five Love Languages, developed by Dr. Gary Chapman. All the couples I have coached appreciate each part of the process, but most agree that the Love Languages part represents the most practical and useful tool for daily marriage improvement. Once you apply this knowledge, expect progress!

Team-Building

No, you will not be asked to do a "trust fall" or to solve some puzzle together. This type of team-building looks intently at how each partner approaches some of the most important functions of the relationship. The goal will be to agree on how to "do marriage" by uncovering hidden assumptions and identifying expectations.

In couples coaching, I use the PREPARE/ENRICH Inventory. This thirty-five-year-old inventory has been used by over four million couples, benefits from vast research from its couple database, and is available in twelve languages, so is cross-culturally relevant. One version of the Inventory may be used with an individual couple and another shorter version fits group settings, like retreats.

In chapter 8 I will introduce you to several of the ten important issues addressed by the inventory. If you wish to attend a retreat or schedule your own PREPARE/ENRICH Inventory, contact me or one of 100,000 other trained facilitators worldwide! Information will be included in this chapter.

The process wraps up by anticipating some of the barriers slowing progress on Charity Lane, or that tend to cause a detour. You will see that you picked up relational tools along the road that prepare you for the barriers and the potential detours.

Are you ready to explore marriage together on the less-traveled road?

CHAPTER 4:

Where Happiness Follows

Y ou want to recapture happiness in your marriage. I know marriage happiness awaits you, but not by turning back the hands of time and not by retracing your earlier steps on Happiness Boulevard.

I want to show you the path to this happiness you seek. Are you ready for it? In a nutshell, you can realize happiness in your marriage if you do marriage God's way. Fully stated: If you do marriage God's way with God's help, you receive God's results: a purposeful and passionate marriage that experiences significant happiness as a by-product of God's purpose and passion at work in the relationship.

Human happiness cannot sustain a marriage. I know, it seemed to do so pretty well early on, right? Yet, it faded or your search would not have led you here. To make the point even clearer, neither can sex, nor security, nor money found a lasting marriage. A marriage that withstands the pressures and problems of life rests securely on God's purpose and finds itself fueled by God's love.

Let me show you what doing marriage God's way and with God's help means. The next three chapters will give you the lay of the land along Charity Lane. Walk with me as I show you.

Engineering Charity Lane

To thoroughly understand God's way in marriage, I need to take you back to the blueprints. They're archived in Heaven's D.O.T. While I can't take you to Heaven, I can direct you to the story we humans were given about the initial planning and construction of Charity Lane. You'll find the story in the first two chapters of the Bible, Genesis 1 and 2. Listen as I retell the salient points for you.

In the great Engineering Hall of Heaven, God gathered a team to help design and build the universe in space and time – Genesis 1. As we enter the story God surveys a dark, swirling, watery mass. Let's just assume that God and the team produced this raw material as the first matter in the new three-dimensional space.

Next, God acted on the raw material. He spoke galaxies into existence: Let there be... and He named something new. Immediately the words acted on the raw material to begin ordering and enlivening it. Step-by-step God called our world into existence, everything except us humans. He saved humans for last. We became the crowning glory of

God's creative effort. How do we know? We know because we humans alone were created in God's image. Notice Genesis 1, verses 26 and 27, from the Contemporary English Version (CEV):

God said, "Now we will make humans, and they will be like us. We will let them rule the fish, the birds, and all other living creatures." Humanity's divine image showed in dominion over creation. The Creator shared rule over the creation with us human creatures.

This is huge for your marriage and mine because God implied divine intention for human marriage in the decision to create human beings. Look carefully at the pronoun used in the story: "Now we will make humans, and they will be like *us*." (I added the emphasis) God created humans to be like himself; He made men and women. Without rolling out the several complicated linguistic, form, and theological arguments about what this means, just know that very smart people disagree about the meaning of "us." I tend to fall on the theological side of this argument, taking the plural pronoun to mean the God-head, or the Trinity – God, the Father, the Son, and the Holy Spirit.

What difference does it make? Simply this: God presents as a community of three-in-one. The Trinity chose to create humanity in duality, as male and female, to be a representation of the divine community. The divine community lives in unity, "let us." The divine community expresses benevolent creativity, "create men and women." The divine community gives of itself generously without thought of or desire for repayment, "in our image and likeness." The divine community shares sovereign rule, "let them have dominion." Now, imagine a marriage reflecting divine relationship! I believe God imagined it.

Our very desire to marry reflects the image of God. We humans realize our greatest wholeness in the relationship God intended. So, Mary Beth and I as a married couple more closely reflect God's image than either of us do alone.

Are you beginning to see how this understanding reframes marriage? To be created in God's image means to be created with a deep desire for a relationship – created, actually, for divine intimacy.

Maybe you have never put the words "divine" and "intimacy" together. Yet, the intimacy of human marriage was created in the "likeness" of divine intimacy. Read this and I'll explain myself, Genesis 2:21-24 (Contemporary English Version):

> *"So the Lord God made him fall into a deep sleep, and he took out one of the man's ribs. Then after closing the man's side, the Lord made a woman out of the rib. The Lord God brought her to the man, and the man exclaimed, 'Here is someone like me! She is part of my body, my own flesh and bones. She came from me, a man. So I will name her Woman!' That's why a man will leave his own father and mother. He marries a woman, and the two of them become like one person."*

While modern sensitivities often read into this passage some priority of order, male before female, I read a beautiful example of human relationship reflecting divine relationship. I read of human intimacy mirroring divine oneness. The man's exclamation recognized the sameness of woman versus the difference of the animals God created as man's companions. The man realized he could relate to the woman much more profoundly than with the other creatures. His comment reflected a relational intimacy, not just physical intimacy. Oh, that we spouses would look at each other with the wide-eyed wonder of the first man's realization! With the understanding that human marriage reflects the relational intimacy among God, the Father, Son, and Spirit, we may begin to grasp the divine purpose for marriage.

Marriage with Divine Purpose

Genesis 1 and 2 hint at the divine purpose for marriage. In chapter 1, God gives to the couple dominion. They were meant to rule the creation as God would rule. How do I know? They were created in God's image and likeness. God built into their being the capacity to be and to do like their creator. Their rule would not be absolute but found its basis on God's intention for the creation. In other words, God delegated. They understood creation to be God's, not theirs. They understood that God's intention shaped their actions. Adam and Eve were created with a divine destiny. As the offspring of the first humans, we too share that divine destiny and marriage plays an important role in fulfilling it!

So, how could the couple fulfill their divine destiny? Genesis 2:25 lays bare, forgive the pun, the answer: "Although the man and his wife were both naked, they were not ashamed." Sadly, our culture has so perverted human nakedness that we may miss the symbolism. For our purpose of understanding God's purpose for marriage, focus on the lack of shame. The man and woman stood completely transparent to each other. They opened themselves to each other in absolute vulnerability. Even so, the purity of their relationship allowed no shame. They had nothing to hide from each other, or from their Creator.

Yes, that thought sends a shiver, doesn't it? Where and before whom may we stand completely vulnerable and absolutely transparent? Imagine the relational intimacy of such a reality! Most of us cannot. Maybe you have been so wounded by those in whom you placed your trust that you would not. I understand. We all bear wounds that stop us short of baring our souls completely. Some have been wounded so deeply or so young or so often that transparency and vulnerability seem too dangerous. In our woundedness and fear, we construct and substitute a way to be married that we believe to be safer.

Happiness Boulevard exists as a human substitute for Charity Lane. When we humans engineer relationships, we build in safety features to protect us from hurt. We've often seen our parents hurt in marriage, or friends hurt in relationships, and we have felt the sting of another's disloyalty. So, we seek a safe haven in marriage. We construct relationships meant to fulfill our needs. In this safety-seeking, personal need-fulfilling desire, we find the blueprint for Happiness Boulevard.

Traveling Charity Lane leads us to be spiritually, emotionally, and physically "naked" before another person and before God. Here's the point so often missed by those traveling Happiness Boulevard: God purposed for marriage to lead a couple to the profound relational intimacy with each other so that they may be prepared to experience relational intimacy with God. The selfward, meet-my-needs focus of Happiness Boulevard leads us away from deep intimacy with each other and with God.

The intimacy God designed in marriage can exist only in growing transparency and vulnerability. An intimate relationship with God will only exist in growing transparency and vulnerability before Him.

Doing Marriage God's Way

Doing marriage God's way means living in transparency and vulnerability with one's human companion and one's divine companion. Of course, God does not expect us to live transparently or vulnerably with an abusive partner. Love and abuse of any kind never can exist together. If your marriage happiness withered in an abusive relationship, then understand that you can never know what God planned for you in that environment. What's worse, living in abuse warps a person's sense of who they are and who God is. That's a conversation for another space, but an abusive relationship will damage a person to their spiritual core. God can heal those wounds, but not in that environment.

Before us lies a choice between two paths, one of God's design, the other of our design. Humans engineered Happiness Boulevard as a path to self-fulfillment and relative safety. When we ask another person to fill our needs and make us happy, our selfward focus means we tend to risk less. We may remain guarded, less trusting, transparent, and vulnerable. We can shield ourselves from the risk of being hurt. We encounter a problem on Happiness Boulevard: It cannot live up to its name! For the emotion of happiness grows in an environment of trust, transparency, and vulnerability. Happiness cannot grow where shame abounds.

God, on the other hand, engineered Charity Lane to be the path that leads you to the deepest of human relationships and that prepares us for a deep relationship with God. God constructed Charity Lane on a spiritual foundation whereas Happiness Boulevard rests on an emotional foundation. The journey down Charity Lane encourages greater trust, greater transparency, and greater vulnerability with each other, which enables a deepening intimacy. The deepening human intimacy prepares one for greater trust, transparency, and vulnerability with God. God purposed human marriage to help us understand divine/human intimacy. As we grow more trusting, transparent, and vulnerable with God, it becomes more likely we will experience happiness as the byproduct. Now we're talking marriage maximized!

On Happiness Boulevard we set emotional happiness as the goal. We believe and expect our partner will make us happy. If our spouse makes us happy, then everything else will take care of itself, right? By now I hope you see the fallacy of that thinking trail.

God has a better plan. It's not easier, but it's satisfying. It's not less risky, but the results far outweigh the risks. God sets before us Charity Lane as the path to fulfilling love and intimacy. Happiness seems to follow those who find on Charity Lane deepening relationships with each other and with God.

CHAPTER 5:

At Love's Cross Purpose

Genesis 1 and 2 provide a different perspective on marriage from the one dreamed about in adolescence and sought in marriage. God planned for us to travel Charity Lane but we humans built a different perspective and a different path, Happiness Boulevard. With deepening intimacy with our partner and with God as the perspective that promises all that God intended for your marriage, including happiness, we now begin to answer the question: How do we do marriage God's way? What are the first steps on Charity Lane? God demonstrated the kind of love that enables a marriage to be done His way.

To answer those questions, we will take one more look at Genesis and then skip over to the New Testament to complete the story. We will touch on Genesis 3:1-9, then move over to hear what Jesus and Paul can tell us.

Obviously, the state of marriage doesn't reflect the "naked but not ashamed" intimacy seen in Genesis 2:25. Only fifty percent of first marriages in the US survive. Well, in case you didn't know it, the very first marriage lost its luster. Adam and Eve remained married, but they lost the initial transparency and vulnerability.

As we understand their story, we better understand ours. Look at it with me.

Crossing the Line

The first couple lived in a pristine garden. Imagine a place with no artificial noise, no crime, and no pollution. Nice, huh? Only natural beauty, the run of the garden… well, except for that one prohibition. God had put in the middle of the garden a tree, called the Tree of the Knowledge of Good and Evil. God warned the couple to leave that tree's fruit alone.

You may wonder why God would do such a thing. Why place only one prohibition and the prohibited thing in the middle of the garden? The answer reveals much about God's love: If the man and woman did not have a choice, then they could not choose God. Yes, the tree in the middle of the garden represented their ability to choose. It's part of being created in God's image. We'll look more deeply into God's love a bit later. For now, look at the tree as a representation of the free will God gave humans that enables humans to give and receive love.

When you begin reading Genesis 3 you find Eve casting a longing glance at the fruit of this tree. Without going into depth with the conversation she had with the serpent, just know that she and Adam chose the fruit. They crossed the only boundary line set by God. They chose their way over God's way.

No sooner had they savored the sweetness of that fruit did they realize they were naked. In other words, they saw themselves differently.

What was different? They saw the same bodies. Let's summarize it by saying that for the first time they saw each other from a self-centered point-of-view. God's purpose for human intimacy – to prepare one for divine/human relationship – had been supplanted by a human desire for personal fulfillment and personal gratification.

We've seen the results of this decision. It may have escaped notice, but this self-centered point-of-view subtly expresses itself in a comment heard often at weddings, "I love him because he's always there for me!" We cringe when we encounter the fully-fruited expression of selfishness found in the objectifying of another as seen in pornography.

These comments may shock you. I mean no judgment, nor do I accuse. Yet, we cannot ignore the ugly potential of wanting a way different from the benevolent intention of God.

God wants you to experience deepening relationships with both Him and your spouse. Even so, intimacy as God planned cannot grow and blossom fully in self-centeredness. Finding your maximum marriage depends on an understanding of why Happiness Boulevard leads us in the wrong direction. If you realize that your marriage presently travels Happiness boulevard, fret not.

Good News

Something's missing in most marriages, namely doing marriage God's way. Good news, though, God hasn't left us to stew in our own selfish pot. Instead, God loves us still. God chose to redeem us, meaning God offers us another opportunity for a relationship with each other and with Him. There's hope for a good marriage on *Charity Lane*.

To hear that good news, let's skip forward to the New Testament and to weeks before Jesus' crucifixion. Knowing the meaning of Jesus' life, death, and resurrection for your life as an individual is great but let me ask you this question: have you ever considered the implications of Jesus' teaching and action for your marriage?

God's plan for redemption arrived as a Spirit-sired child to a virgin, single mother, whose fiancé was a carpenter. No matter how common and unremarkable today we find birth out of wedlock, such an event in that culture would have proven scandalous and marked the mother and the child for life.

This child drew his first human breath in an unusual place for a birth that carried the odors of a barn. On that baby's grown-up shoulders would rest the fate of the world in the form of a cross. God sent His son to lead the Way back to an eternal relationship with Him and enduring relationship with each other. God allowed His son, Jesus, to bear the consequences of our human self-centeredness: No less than eternal separation from God. Jesus would take that cross, which was the cruelest form of punishment the Roman government could render, and accept the consequences of our separation from God in our stead.

You may shrink back from the idea that God allowed Jesus to stand in your place in punishment for selfishness. Yet, at the very beginning God set boundaries for a relationship. Those boundaries remain in place for us as well. Once a person chooses to cross that line – chooses his or her own way over God's – the person outside the line may not return. We simply cannot return to a right relationship with God by our own effort. God, as the Celestial Judge, honors that decision, but also enforces the consequence, which is eternal separation. God cannot break His own rules and remain who He is.

That's the bad news. The cross of Jesus renders very good news, God's choice to absorb into Himself the consequences of our willful and selfish decisions. Jesus did that for us! The horror of the crucifixion speaks both of the horrible eternal consequences of our state of separation from God and of the depth of God's love for us. As John's Gospel put it (John 3:16): *God so loved the world that he gave his only son so that whoever believes in him shall not die* (i.e., be eternally separated) *but will have eternal life*. God loves you, wants you to share His life, and intends for your marriage, done His way, to lead you into a deepening intimacy with your spouse and with Him.

Done His Way

To be done His way, we need to hear Jesus invite the disciples to follow Him to the cross. We hear the invitation in Luke 9:23 (The Voice Translation): "If any of you want to walk My path, you're going to have to *deny yourself.* You'll have to *take up your cross every day* and *follow me.* If you try to avoid danger and risk, then you'll lose everything. If you let go of your life and risk all for My sake, then your life will be rescued, *healed, made whole and full"* (emphasis added). Jesus' sacrifice redeemed individuals but his cross also held God's purpose for marriage.

Have you heard this passage read before? Have you yourself read it? I suspect that no matter how many times you have heard or read this passage, no matter how many sermons you may have heard on this passage, you never heard it applied to marriage. Hear Jesus calling all would-be followers to three actions: deny, take up daily, follow. Let us apply this passage to our marriage as we go.

Deny Self addresses the need for humility. The first action addresses the self-centered and willful streak running through each of us. Denying self-amounts to humbling oneself before our Creator. Eve and Adam gave up humility for their disobedience. The self-sacrificial act of denying self puts a person in the condition to choose God's will again and to be redeemed. When you and I deny self, then we have put ourselves in a condition for

God to recover His divine purpose for our life *and* for our marriage.

Take Up the Cross Daily speaks to adopting God's purpose. Humanity lost its God-given purpose of co-regency over creation when we ate the fruit of our will and way. To take up the cross implies our humble acceptance of God's purpose of redeeming humanity revealed in Jesus' humble obedience and sacrifice. As we will see later, God folds marriage into His redemptive purpose for the world. Charity Lane leads its partnered pilgrims to greater depths of humble obedience and sacrifice.

Follow Me invites us to travel the Way of Love. Jesus' journey to Golgotha blazed the path of Love. Not a sentimental journey. Not an emotional journey. A volitional journey. Jesus chose to take up our cross. He could have chosen a self-centered and less painful path. He counted the costs to himself and the benefits accrued for all by his obedience. He *chose* the cross. He accepted God's purpose for his death. He trusted God would redeem us after He raised Jesus. The Good News still resounds: We have been redeemed because of Jesus' humble, purposeful sacrifice on our behalf.

How Does This Apply to Marriage?

You want to know why this will help you find your happiness. Consider the following:

1. Humility puts ego (self) back in its proper place in relationship to God. It's a place of humility.

Marriage as God intended calls for the regular discipline of denying self so that we are able to embrace God's purpose for marriage. Eating the fruit of selfishness turns one in a direction moving away from God, therefore away from God's purpose. The self-centered life faces away from God; the humble life turns toward God. The self-centered life seeks its own gratification; the humble life becomes able to sacrifice self for God's divine purpose. Humility allows God's will to be accomplished in a marriage as both partners face God together.

2. The cross brings the divine purpose back to the marriage relationship. The believing/following woman of Jesus understands God sets her as the primary instrument of redemption in her spouse's life! Likewise, if the man is going to love his bride as Jesus loved, then he willingly sacrifices so that God's will may be accomplished in her life.

This humble sacrifice in order that God's will be accomplished in another's life defines God's love. This is the only love that will accomplish God's will in marriage and in the world!

Love as revealed in Jesus' life and death is the only love that God can use in our marriages to accomplish His divine purpose for us and through us. The cross expresses God's creative love redemptively. The same love that prompted God to create us in His image and share with us dominion over His creation prompted God to pay our debt for disobedience to reestablish us to an eternal relationship with Him.

We may accurately say that marriage God's way exists with a "cross" purpose. The way to accomplish God's cross purpose in marriage involves denying self, taking up daily God's purpose for your spouse, and following through to the end that purpose on earth. Even though denying self and sacrificing for your spouse stood front-and-center in this chapter, we haven't forgotten happiness. Remember Jesus' words in The Voice Translation of Luke 9:25? "If you let go of your life and risk all for My sake, then your life will be rescued, *healed, made whole and full.*" Paraphrased and applied to marriage happiness, Jesus' words sound like this: "If you humbly deny yourself for the sake of God's will to be done in your spouse's life, then you will experience marriage rescued, healed, made whole and full – including happiness."

The "cross" purpose accepted and applied takes the marriage to the next level—marriage maximized.

CHAPTER 6

Love Divine, All Loves Excelling

Let's pick up the love-thread from the last chapter. God loves you. You may well agree, but just because we agree does not mean we think similarly about God's love. The English language actually hides as much as it reveals about love, especially God's love. For example, without confusing you I can say that I love my wife, I love pizza, I love my children, I love our pet dog Myrtle, I love playing softball. You realize that our English word *love* allows different expressions. Even so, on occasion, our single word for love provides too little information.

According to the Greek language used in the New Testament, you actually may love four different ways. The New Testament language contained four different words that our one English language translates as "love." Only one of those words captures divine love as revealed in Jesus. It's the one that leads a couple to do marriage God's way and to realize the results God intended.

The most familiar Greek word for love spoke of love between man and woman, *eros*. Yes, it sounds familiar because our English word *erotic* passes directly from Greek to English. This word now carries more negative freight than the Greeks understood. While *eros* denoted what we today often label *erotica*, it also described the healthy physical intimacy between spouses.

When the Greeks wished to describe kindness or brotherly love, they employed the word, *philadelphos*. Don't you hear the name of the American city, Philadelphia, the city of brotherly love? This compound Greek word combines a word for *friendship* or *affection* with the word for *brother*. The Greek word refers to the value and affection that dear friends share, as today we may refer to someone as our BF. Very similar ideas.

A third Greek term refers directly to family relationships, *storgē*, pronounced *stōr- gā*. This Greek word describes how you love your aunts and uncles, cousins, and grandparents. It's a healthy affection for relatives.

The first three Greek loves contain emotional significance. The fourth Greek term, *agapē* (ä-gä-pä), rests primarily on the foundation of will. Instead of describing emotion, this word describes a volition. Now, let's return to John 3:16: "God loved (*agapē*) the world so much that he gave..." God's will to rescue us lay behind the decision to allow Jesus to take our place in eternal separation. Jesus' will to obey His Father enabled him to embrace the cross instead of his fear of the cross' great pain.

With the decision-based love in mind, we may return to the cross as God's picture of divine love reflected in the two-become-one relationship. God created us humans in this decision-based love existing in the three-in-one relationship we understand to be God. God's love involves the sacrifice of one, in this case, the Son, on behalf of another, the Father, so that God's best may be accomplished in our life. In the crucifixion, God allowed Jesus to be sacrificed in order that we may be eternally rescued.

Since God created us in the divine image, and since the sacrifice on the cross perfectly pictures God's love, then it makes sense that God intended a selfless, sacrificial love in marriage to weld a couple into one. *Agapē* is the foundation of marriage as God intended. *Agapē* alone defines divine love. *Eros* serves a secondary role to *agapē*.

We humans, on the other hand, gravitate toward the physically-based love, don't we? *Eros* may very well contain a genuine affection for another. Your *eros* may seek good physical and emotional intimacy with your companion, but it does not pivot on a decision to sacrifice so that God's best be accomplished in your spouse's life. At its best, *eros* represents a non-manipulative emotional desire for another person. Less than its best, *eros* uses another person for selfish purposes. At its worst, *eros* objectifies another human being for one's sordid gratification.

Happiness Boulevard by default defines the best love in terms of *eros*. According to God's design, marriage on Charity Lane thrives on *agapē*.

The love of the cross accepted by a couple brings a profound shift in marriage's purpose. God created us for relationship characterized by divine love, or *agapē*. How does this apply to marriage? Glad you asked. We now begin to turn a corner in both principle and practice.

The Paradigm Shifts Here

The distinction between a relationship based on the physical love of *eros* and the spiritual love of *agapē* may be seen as the difference between seeking personal happiness and seeking to serve another in marriage. Human love focuses primarily on self; spiritual love, as defined by God on the cross, focuses on others. *Eros* tends to be self-centered. *Agapē* centers attention on others and being used to accomplish God's will for and in them.

Getting Practical

The Apostle Paul attempted to apply God's spiritual love to relationships. In both Ephesians 5:21-6:9 and Colossians 3:18-4:1 Paul described the difference *agapē* would make in the complex of family relationships.

Viewed through twenty-first-century cultural lenses, Paul's writing appears to be restrictively patriarchal. For years my mother thought Paul a braggart and a chauvinist. After years of study and prayer, she now realizes that Paul offered revolutionary advice from the perspective of the first-century middle-eastern family structure. If you discounted Paul as relationally backward, then give me a moment to offer an explanation.

For example, in both the Ephesian and the Colossian passages Paul redefined the relationship of masters and slaves. He counseled each to treat the other in light of their relationship to God in Christ. If the master and the slave both followed Christ, they were also brothers in Christ. The master/slave relationship would be temporary. The kin-in-Christ relationship would last for eternity! Therefore, slaves obey your masters as though you were obeying Christ, and masters treat your slaves as your Master, Christ, treated you – think the cross! That's radical.

We believe slavery to be inhumane. Yet, we do not live with socially and governmentally sanctioned slavery either. Paul took the accepted relational standards of his day and applied a radical way of viewing those relationships that were based on God's divine love, or *agapē*. Viewed from Paul perspective, he proposed a radical shift in the relationship between master and slave/slave and master.

Paul's redefinition of the husband/wife relationship proved no less transformative. In a patriarchal culture that fostered in men a superiority complex and engendered a lack of respect for women, Paul sought to infuse *agapē*. Once again, let's attempt to remove the lenses of our post-suffrage and feminist-conditioned culture and see things as Paul addressed them. To the congregations receiving his letters, Paul's advice seemed counter-intuitive to minds conditioned by cultural and legal patriarchy. Let me explain briefly by using Paul's family advice in the letter to the Ephesian believers.

One Surprising Word

Let's consider Ephesians 5:21-33. For a clearer understanding, I will explain a bit of the background to this passage. Paul knew many of the Ephesian believers well. He'd spent two-and-a-half to three years building the congregations in and around Ephesus. His letter may have been written for several congregations in Ephesus and in neighboring towns.

Paul followed a pattern in his letters: a brief greeting – teaching section – application section – finally, concluding comments and directions for individuals. In this letter, after the greeting, Paul taught the believers how to be the Church and how to relate to each other and the non-believing world (chapters 1-3). Midway through, Paul shifted to practical application (chapter 4-6). His practical advice covered the typical family of that time, which often included the married couple, children, sometimes parents, and in many instances, house slaves (5:21-6:9).

Verse 21 of this passage serves as an umbrella under which the remainder of the passages were covered: "Submit to one another out of reverence for Christ" (New International Version). Focus first on the word *submit*.

Paul borrowed a familiar military term to frame his advice to all family members. The word we translate from Greek as *submit* literally means *to order under*. Picture soldiers rousted out of sleep and told to "fall in!" You'd see a number of soldiers running to a position facing their leader, spacing themselves in horizontal and vertical rows, standing at attention. Paul chose to apply that kind of instant obedience to all relationships.

Next, he applied the concept to everyone, even the men who were the undisputed family leaders. I suspect the adult male hearers of the letter were quite surprised to hear Paul counsel that they *order under* wives, children, and slaves! Again, Paul wrote radical advice.

Finally, in verse 21 Paul identified the motivation for such humble behavior – reverence, or respect, for their Lord. Son Jesus' submission to Father God and his accepting crucifixion to pay our debt to God's standard of relationship serve as the motivation for a couple to mutually submit. This submission does not act according to the social mores, but according to the spiritual model seen in Jesus. Notice how deeply this divine love affects individual and cultural life! Paul's direction would radically change the direction of ancient marriages. For us today, Paul's advice calls for a shift in our "enlightened" twenty-first-century marriages from Happiness Boulevard to Charity Lane.

Take this contemporary example. The *agapē* of God at work in a twenty-first- century wife will transform her identity as a woman and a wife. Women have been held down for millennia. I am an only brat who was reared by a single mom. I witnessed her work much harder than men to secure lesser jobs. I watched auto mechanics take advantage of her because she didn't know the inner workings of cars. I saw her passed over for jobs that were given to men with lesser skills. When she began to crack the glass ceiling, I watched her excel over all men before her in this position except her immediate supervisor. I believe in equal pay for equal work! I believe women and men should be valued and treated equally in the workplace!

Our era of greater equality provides women the opportunity to stretch their wings. The call today for women's empowerment does address inequities in our culture; however, in marriage, the lure of empowerment stands 180° away from mutual submission. Empowerment seeks equality, but equality based on power. Mutual submission in Christ leads to true equality – equality of selfless sacrifice. Ordering under another means getting over self! Jesus got over himself the Garden of Gethsemane to order under God's will. By getting over himself, Jesus could get under and take up his cross so he could lift us up to God.

God's *agapē* also transforms the twenty-first-century husband. God calls husbands to forsake the influence of our culture and to allow God to shape their thinking and their relating, especially to their wives. For example, men have been told that they need to be self-sufficient – to John-Wayne-it through life. Unfold that idea of self-sufficiency. It's self-focused. It fosters separation from others, lest one become dependent on another. It overestimates an individual's resources and abilities, as if men may meet any and all circumstances alone.

Such self-sufficiency leads away from God's purpose and intention. It will not allow for humility or dependence, which rest at the foundation of a healthy relationship with God. In fact, God calls husbands to become humbly dependent on Him in order to accomplish God's purpose in marriage. How can God's selfless, sacrificial love pour through a selfish, prideful channel? Too narrow and too shallow! God's selfless love cannot flow through a self-dependent channel, because selfishness and pride will not *order under* and reach low enough to channel God's love.

Truly, God's way calls husbands to the hero's place. That said, think about what heroes say about their actions. The hero almost always admits to being no one special (humility). The hero goes on to say that he didn't think of himself in the action, but of the other person (selfless service). The hero didn't stop to count the cost but committed completely no matter what the cost (sacrificial). The words may differ, but heroes often speak this way.

God calls husbands to the heroic action of divinely-enabled, humble, selfless, sacrificial service for the sake of wives. Only this brand of heroism fulfills God's purpose and intention for marriage. Only this brand of heroism creates an atmosphere for enduring marriage that knows happiness too!

To sum it up: *Agapē* calls for equality in marriage – not equal power, but *equal submission*, or *equal powerlessness*! Paul's application of divine love remains radical in the twenty-first century, calling men from the hubris of self-sufficiency and women from the hubris of living "empowered" lives. Uh oh, I didn't just say that, did I?! I did, and I totally believe we twenty-first-century men and women need correction as much as the first-century men and women. In applying *agapē* to marriage, if a man chafes at the thought of moving from self-sufficiency or a woman from empowerment, then hubris has reared its head and its "cultural curls" likely need spiritual straightening.

One final, crucial thought to add here: only God can supply to you and me the divine love required for us to *order under* our spouses. Divine love is just that. Its source comes from God. We do not have it in us. It's not human love. Roughly speaking, human love fuels our trip on Happiness Boulevard; divine love fuels our journey down Charity Lane. Many well-meaning travelers seek to develop solid and wonderful relationships on Happiness Boulevard and some people do better than others. Yet, to do marriage God's way you need God's help, meaning you and I need God, the Holy Spirit, indwelling, informing, empowering, guiding, gracing us to humble ourselves, and enabling us to forgive and seek forgiveness.

Charity Lane in View

Let's begin to assemble the pieces of the last three chapters. You and I want happy marriages. God wants us to know happiness too, but His way differs from the human way. We circle back to the overarching understanding of marriage from God's perspective: If we do marriage God's way (selfless, sacrificial, ordering-under love) with God's help (the indwelling Spirit providing *agapē*) then we can realize God's results–a maximized marriage, imbued with a divinely purposeful and passionate relationship which experiences significant and lasting happiness as the byproduct.

With that thought in mind, can you begin to see why Happiness Boulevard can never lead to the same relationship as Charity Lane? Where is the focus of the couple on Happiness Boulevard? On how my spouse can make me happy. Generally speaking, thoughts about God's will for the marriage find little room on Happiness Boulevard.

Traveling on Charity Lane implies a continual awareness of God's presence and God's purpose. As Frost would pen, *that makes all the difference*!

The road less traveled, or the way to realize the marriage God desires for you, reflects the divine relationship within the human relationship. It leads each partner to *deny self, take up God's purpose daily* for one's spouse, and to *follow through to the end*. Practically speaking, that selfless sacrifice on behalf of our partner means a Spirit-enabled *ordering under* each other out of respect for Jesus' sacrifice. On Charity Lane, the traveling couple never loses sight of God, the divine purpose for marriage, the divine love necessary to fulfill that purpose, and the expression of that love through lowering self under our partner to lift him or her up to God.

Let me assure you, the act of denying self under God for His will to be accomplished in your partner's life paradoxically offers the only way to experience lasting and significant happiness God intended in marriage. Let's now look at how you can begin to do marriage God's way with God's help to receive God's maximizing results, including happiness.

CHAPTER 7:

Personality: From Perceived Weaknesses to Potential Strengths

Those early weeks of new love felt magical. Mary Beth's beauty took my breath away each time I met her. She acted so very polite and related to everyone with a fetching kindness. Her vocal performances shocked me with their strength and professional quality when I first heard her sing. Her spirit matched mine and we shared the same values. I even found her quietness intriguing, especially since my mouth rarely rested. We could carry on a conversation for hours, but when she found herself in a group of four or more, she listened much more than she talked. I assumed she was just a bit shy and I was confident that I could bring her out of that!

I envisioned "rescuing" her from her shyness. As her tall, dark, and naïve knight in rusty armor, I expected to be able to transform her into a talkative, out-there person just like me! But love would conquer all, right?

Do you remember those first weeks and months of new love? Do you remember the alluring mysteries and exciting discoveries about your love interest? At first, almost everything new seemed exciting and wonderful. Then with time, you began to realize that your beloved had a few peculiarities. Perhaps you too thought you'd help him or her to change. You felt confident about that. Then those early impressions were seasoned with experience. The rose-colored glasses of infatuation gave way to the clean-lensed reality that you loved a real person, who possessed real differences from you. You began to realize that you could not change your lover to fit your ideal partner. Yet, you loved on, wondering what to do now that your initial picture had changed.

Take heart. With a bit of understanding and a dose of acceptance, I hope you find that those peculiarities you feared to be weaknesses in your marriage may actually be transformed into strengths. You supply the acceptance, I'll supply the understanding and I'll keep it simple.

The Myer-Briggs Type Indicator

This long-established and very helpful inventory present four "dichotomies" of personal preferences: Extraversion (E) and Introversion (I) – notice that in their writing, Katharine and Isabel spelled the E preference "extraversion," not "extroversion"; Sensing (S) and Intuition (N – using the second letter so as not to be confused with Introversion); Thinking (T) and Feeling (F); Judging (J) and Perceiving (P). Each preference sits at the end of a scale with the mid-point set at zero (0) with the value toward each end increasing to an end-point of 100. It looks like this:

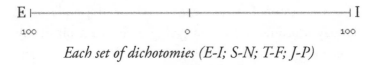

Each set of dichotomies (E-I; S-N; T-F; J-P)
is set as a scale like this.

The result of the inventory yields a four-letter type and the strength of each letter, based on where responses fall on the scale. For example, my latest personality results look like this: ENFJ Extravert (69%) iNtuitive (69%) Feeling (66%) Judging (25%). I show a distinct preference of extraversion over introversion; a distinct preference for intuition; a distinct preference for feeling; and a moderate preference for judging over perceiving.

To understand the pairs of preferences, think about them this way:

Favorite World—E & I

Do you prefer to focus on the outer world or on your own inner world? This is called Extraversion (E) or Introversion (I), respectively. Here's how I explain this preference pair to couples. Each of us possesses only so much energy to focus on your world–imagine a ball of energy the size of a basketball. Now, as an extravert, I will spread that energy over a broad group of people. Of course, the more persons I give some of that energy, the less I have to give each one. An introvert takes that energy and sinks it into fewer people. Many introverts actually have only four or five really close friends, but they invest much more energy into each relationship.

As a pastor, I would engage scores of people on a Sunday morning. I enjoyed giving each one a bit of my love-energy. I knew something about each one and sought to learn more. That served me well as I served congregations of increasing size over my ministry.

Another feature of extraversion and introversion describes how one thinks. As an extravert, I think best as I think out loud. The words I hear from myself help me to think better than the thought that remain bottled inside. On the other hand, an introvert finds talking out loud about something actually impedes the thinking process. An introvert will withdraw to an internal deliberation chamber and noodle through an issue before speaking about it.

Information—S & N

Do you prefer to focus on the basic information you take in or do you prefer to interpret and add meaning? This is called Sensing (S) or Intuition (N), respectively. Sensing prefers gathering information through the five senses. Makes sense! This preference means that the sensor takes in pieces of information, studies them, and places them in an order. They are linear thinkers, taking in, examining, and placing in a row each bit of information. The sensors often demonstrate keen powers of observation, like Sherlock Holmes. They also will be overwhelmed if they receive too much sensory information at one time. Consequently, when a sensor is listening to a conversation rich in detail, she may lose some of the content because she stopped to examine an interesting piece of information while the conversation continued. Once the sensor emerges from the examination process, she realizes that the story continued, and she missed a few seconds.

The intuitive gathers information differently. Much research has been and is being done on the process of intuition. Here's the best I've read (though I cannot remember where or by whom): intuitives still receive stimuli from their senses, but this information makes its way much faster through the brain and without the examination. This capacity has little to do with intelligence but more to do with the wiring of the brain. So the information is received so quickly that it appears to be a feeling. A strong intuitive can "read a room" when walking in and realize something of the emotional atmosphere, or can "read a person" and have a feeling about that person. This quick reception of information and quick judgment we call leaping to a conclusion. An intuitive may often be correct but he may also take that leap over an unseen cliff. Those consequences are never good!

Another aspect of intuition describes thinking in big concepts versus the sensor observing small details. Intuitives live in a conceptual stratosphere. They enjoy taking in lots of information about new concepts, then connecting the dots between concepts for which there may not seem to others like obvious connections. While the ability to handle a large volume of information serves intuitives well, living with one's head in the clouds may prove impractical. The view is great, but the oxygen is thin up there!

Decisions—T & F

When making decisions, do you prefer to first look at logic and consistency (T) or first look at the people and special circumstances (F)? This preference pair may be the most self-explanatory. Thinking speaks of making a decision based on an analysis. Thinkers tend to live with concrete reality. Something is right or it's wrong. For you older readers, it's *Dragnet*'s Joe Friday, "Just the facts, ma'am." Thinkers also seem less given to mood changes and less given to expressing emotion. Thinkers do feel and feel deeply, but they prefer living in the world of reason and analysis. The stronger the preference, meaning the further from the zero-point, the more difficulty the thinker may have expressing feelings. Because of living most often in the land of facts, the thinker may come across as cold and unfeeling.

As black and white thinkers, these people will expect everyone to follow every logical rule. No fudging. They sound rigid and seem harsh to feelers, but you may be assured they hold themselves to the same standard.

The feelers make decisions based on relationships. I explain the difference to couples this way. Imagine you were out eating dinner with a couple of friends – one a thinker and one a feeler. Say you ordered a salad. Your friends notice that a piece of spinach stuck to one of your front teeth and it stayed! Now, your thinker friend would lean forward and whisper, "You have spinach on your tooth." Why? Because it's embarrassing and they would want someone to tell them. It's the right thing to do. Your feeler friend decides not to say anything because telling you may embarrass you! The feeler would not want to hurt your feelings. Here lies the crux of the feeler's decision-making: do what seems best for the relationship at the moment.

Just as thinkers can feel, feelers can think. When a feeler thinks, she or he prefers to consider the impact of a decision on the relationship. Feelers may withhold truth deemed hurtful. Feelers tell little white lies, "Oh, yes, that looks nice on you!" even when the clothing fails to flatter. So, the feeler values relationships most highly; the thinker values the truth and what seems correct most highly. Are you beginning to see the potential?

Structure—J & P

In dealing with the outside world, do you prefer to get things decided (J) or do you prefer to stay open to new information and options (P)?

Judgers must not be confused with judgmental people. They may or may not be excessively critical. Instead, this title describes a person who likes decisiveness, who plans, and is future-oriented. The Judger deals with the world in a structured manner. This person likes to build the structure and accomplish things. The judger displays self-discipline. The planning may be thorough but will take no longer than necessary to make a decision and get moving. Because of this, the judger may be seen as rigid and opinionated by the perceiver.

If you prefer a judging attitude toward the world, then you likely live by a calendar, which is planning months out. You love a To-Do list. If you score a distinctive preference for judging, then I suspect the first thing on your daily To-Do list is "write a To-Do list" because you love to mark items off.

I can tell if you have a distinctive judging attitude by looking at your pantry or closet. All labels in your pantry will be turned out so you can read the spice names. In your closet, you likely have all your pants in one section, all shirts or blouses in another, and all your dresses hung together. Your shoes will be lined neatly. You may go far enough as to coordinate colors in your closet, with blues together, whites together, browns and grays and blacks each in their own section! It's just who you are.

Perceivers feel as if the judger's decisive and ordered and structured world feels too restrictive. The perceiver likes more fluidity. She likes to keep options open and wants to gather more information before any decision.

In that way, the perceiver appears more flexible than the judger. Perceivers often fly by the seat of their pants but they usually make a clean landing. At work, perceivers may put off decision-making in favor of more research or more exploration of the issues.

A perceiver will be an in-the-moment person. Perceivers make excellent counselors precisely because of their ability to suspend decisions in favor of walking with you through the problem. Perceivers don't see the need for the structure so valued by the judger. Perceivers need freedom and flow. The perceiver's love of freedom and flow comes across to the judger as a bit aimless and, oh, so indecisive.

Putting the Pieces Together

With a very simple explanation of the MBTI, let's apply this to marriage. Instead of using a hypothetical situation, hear how this changed my marriage.

My Myers-Briggs type, ENFJ, and Mary Beth's, ISFJ, seem similar. We share a distinctive preference for feeling in decision-making. We also share the judging preference, with Mary Beth's J being very mild and mine being moderately strong. We significantly differ in our favorite world, extraversion/introversion, and information gathering, sensing/intuition. For the sake of simplicity, I will address the letters in their sequence and the implications/applications for our marriage maximization.

As an introvert, Mary Beth converses easily with me under normal circumstances, as she does with her few really close friends. The need to turn inward reveals itself primarily when she finds herself in a group of three or more friends, or two or more strangers. She listens much more than she speaks in most of those circumstances.

As an extravert I find talking with a group of friends comfortable and fun. I even strike up conversations with strangers – something my bride will rarely do. As with most extraverts, I have a broad range of relationships, but they are not very deep, except with family. My sweet introvert has a narrow range of relationships, but they are very deep.

In principle, these differences seem benign. In real life, they caused difficulties. As a pastor, whenever we had a congregational gathering, or when she and I attended a community event, our E/I differences created tension. I naturally gravitated toward greeting everyone, catching up on their latest news, and sharing ours. Mary Beth would rather stand or sit near the periphery and talk to whoever came to us. You see it coming, don't you?

I'd walk a few steps away to greet someone, leaving my bride standing alone. (She *hates* to be alone in a crowd!) That conversation led to another a few steps further away, which led to another and another. Soon, I found myself on one side of the room having fun talking with folks while Mary Beth stood on the other side feeling very much forgotten by her husband.

Believe me, we engaged in *many* a tense conversation about that scenario. We finally settled on a compromise. When we entered an event or gathering, I would survey the room for persons I wanted or needed to greet and talk to. We would also look for friends with whom Mary Beth felt comfortable talking to. I would tell her that I wanted/needed to talk to so-and-so and asked if she'd like to go with me or go talk to our friends. She then chose to go with me or for me to drop her off by our friends. I was able to make my contacts without abandoning my beauty by the door. This arrangement worked for us. A better understanding of each other and an appreciation of each other's unique personality needs afforded and affords us a stronger, more confident, less conflicted marriage.

The second set of preferences, sensing and intuition, measure how we gather information. Mary Beth, the sensor, consciously gathers information from the five senses, observes it, and places it carefully as if piecing together a puzzle. Her intentional gathering, her observation of detail, and her careful placing of information require time. Sensors operate best when they can control the rate of information coming to them. If they can pause the flow long enough to consider the new pieces of information, they follow a conversation well. If too much novel information rushes toward them, they catch what they can, observe the detail, place it in the proper order, then return for more. In the meantime, the conversation has continued and parts of the flow slid past uncaptured.

Now, imagine placing my beloved introverted sensor in conversation with me, a distinctive intuitive and an extravert who loves to learn and discuss novel ideas. My dear wife has new-to-her ideas flying toward and past her in Gatling-gun fashion. I'm floating around in the clouds of theory as my poor wife tries to capture, observe, and organize the seemingly disparate thoughts I dump on her.

Now, add to this scene the fact that my strong intuitive personality bent means I'm always cogitating on some idea. I add to our communication difficulties by including Mary Beth in my thinking mid-thought, as if she has been in the conversation from the beginning. Only a mind reader could know what I'm talking about!

The MBTI allows us to identify the communication gap related to her sensing or my intuition. For example, we may be discussing a conversation about a friend. A lull occurs and my mind shifts to another subject. I begin talking about this other subject as if Mary Beth heard everything I've been thinking. So she frequently looks at me with her head tilted, asking something like, "Are we still talking about so-and-so, or is this a new subject?" At least she understands me and responds kindly and without the frustration she would have felt without this understanding—at least, most of the time!

Likewise, I may be sharing some grand new idea or theory. I know she needs a few moments to process the information. When she misses some salient point, I feel less frustrated and can fill in her gaps.

Anytime a couple can increase understanding and appreciation and anytime they can reduce frustration, they will endure less conflict!

Since we share the feeling preference, we understand the process of relational decision-making. Here's a thought. Since neither of us prefers the thinking preference, neither of us experiences the challenge to see the more logical and analytical side of decision-making. Of course, we consider ourselves logical people, but we will choose tact over fact every time! Sometimes we somewhat impoverish our decision-making because of the tact preference.

Likewise, we both share the judging preference. How much stronger would our relationship be if at least one of us balanced the controlled, planned, calendared, future-focused lifestyle with more spontaneity, flexibility, change-tolerance, now-focus!

Our personality difference does not make life easier. Yet, when we understand and appreciate the differences, then we find our marriage stronger. Take as one example, financial decisions. Since we understand each other's strengths, we make better financial decisions. If we need to make a large purchase, I do the research. I love it! I bring the research to Mary Beth with a tentative recommendation. I know that she will look at the material in far greater detail – she's the detail observer; I'm the big picture person. When she's given adequate time and not rushed, Mary Beth will almost always have questions I did not ask, or see negatives I never considered. We make better decisions.

On the other hand, as both a strong intuitive and stronger judger, I am more decisive than she. If we're pressed to make a quick decision, I may not see all she sees, but the time pressure flusters her. So, I generally make the very quick decisions.

The Takeaway

First, your relationship will greatly demystify if you and your spouse together take a Myers-Briggs personality test. You can take the Kersey Temperament Sorter for free online and you can find more than enough explanation of the results. It's a good place to begin understanding each other's God-given and unique personalities. You and your spouse may share a somewhat similar personality. You may discover you possess very different personalities from each other. If not understood, these differences may present small frustrations or may feel like huge barriers. However, when understood and appreciated, these differences may actually strengthen your relationship!

When a couple can accept God's direction in bringing them together and see those differences as fleshing out a more complete picture of the three-in-one community in the two-become-one marriage, then the extra effort pays rich dividends. Marriage maximized!

CHAPTER 8:

Learning Love's Dialects

Love comes in many shades and expressions. To roughly paraphrase Elizabeth Barrett Browning, "How do I love thee? Let me count the ways. I count five, what about you, Robert?" Okay, my poetry needs some waxing before I can wax poetic! Yet, thanks to Gary Chapman, we may count exactly five love languages.

The Five Love Languages

In the early 1990s, Dr. Gary Chapman, an ordained minister and licensed professional counselor, identified five different love languages. These languages may be seen as dialects of the love spoken between two people. The two may be married, or they may be parent and child, or friends, even colleagues. The five dialects do not directly express physical intimacy, though any may eventually lead there. More on that at the end of this chapter.

Chapman describes the five love languages on his website. (Again, at the end of the chapter I will give you information about how to find Dr. Chapman's resources.) As you read these descriptions, you will see yours easily. Ignore yours for now—a practical application of "deny self." *Instead, look for your spouse's love languages.*

Quality Time

This language of love chooses the preposition 'with.' The person whose love language is QT feels most loved with knee-to-knee, nose-to-nose, uninterrupted blocks of time. They need to be the focus of those moments, which means putting down the laptop, muting the TV – better yet, turning off the TV for a few moments – being still, looking at, and listening to your spouse. Eyes and ears demonstrate QT. If you look intently into your spouse's eyes and if you lean into the conversation with your ears, your spouse will feel deeply valued. Of course, 'with' also implies sharing activities together. That includes activities as grand as a vacation to short neighborhood walks together or doing the dinner dishes together. Is your lover one who wants to spend lots of time *with* you?

Acts of Service

The hands best speak Acts of Service love. Lending a hand with housework would be a great expression for the husband whose wife speaks this love language. He may wash and vacuum her car, go to the grocery store, give the kids a bath, or remove and fold clothes from the dryer. The words, "Let me do that for you," will play a symphony to her ears – at least a short love ballad! On the other hand, anything that adds more work to the Acts of Service lover will communicate the opposite. Is your honey the one who really appreciates it when you bring him another cup of coffee?

Words of Affirmation

This lover longs to be valued by the one he/she loves. So, an unsolicited compliment ranks highly. Your WoA husband may not show it outwardly but will smile broadly inwardly when you tell him that he's still your hunk. If you brag on that DIY project he just finished, or how great the car looks after his detailing, or how the yard is the envy of the neighborhood, he will feel so loved. When their special people speak affirming comments, WoA lovers feel deeply valued. You can see that your WoA companion will also be very sensitive to harsh and insulting language. Does your sweetie or your hunk thrive on your genuine praise, encouragement, and affirmation?

Physical Touch

Does your partner grab your hand or take your arm? Does your companion like to sit beside you, give you random hugs and kisses? Does he like his neck or his feet massaged? PT love language speaks as much with touch as with words. Emotional closeness and physical closeness are perceived as one. Yes, physical intimacy means much to the PT lover, but he also wants and needs reassurance of love with the small and incidental touches and kisses. To the PT lover, distance feels like neglect, like punishment. Does your companion long for your touch?

Receiving Gifts

Have you seen your spouse crushed because you forgot an anniversary or a birthday? Likely, he or she feels most loved when receiving gifts. Non-RG lovers may think this love language shallow, until they understand how small gifts carry great weight. The material gift represents time and intention. The small gift says, "Oh, you *were* thinking of me!" The price of the gift does not determine the value of the gift to the RG lover. It's that you took the time and thought through the gift, so that a child's handmade gift may be valued more highly than a piece of jewelry. Does your gift from God get a real kick out of your gifts, even the small ones?

Filling Your Spouse's Love-Tank

In his book *The 5 Love Languages: The Secret to Love that Lasts*, Chapman borrows from a psychiatrist the idea of "filling your spouse's love-tank." When we love our mates in a way they feel most loved, we pump their hearts full of love. Chapman says we can fill our partner's love-tank when we speak their dialect of love. For example, if you speak the dialect of gifts but your partner speaks quality time and you may thoughtfully shower your partner with gifts, then even though your spouse may appreciate the gifts, his or her heart will register very little change on the love fuel gauge! We all need food, as we all need love, but you have a favorite food. If you really love a ribeye steak but you receive chicken or fish every night, you can live! But you will not love the meals. Likewise, if your partner speaks quality time, he or she may appreciate gifts, but will not feel loved as much as by your offering quality time. Speaking something other than our beloved's primary love language will compare to pulling your spouse's care into the gas station on a near-empty tank and only washing the windshield. It's appreciated but it won't get them very far!

The goal of the *5 Love Languages* focuses on your spouse's love language, not yours. To communicate love with your spouse, you need to know his language and know how to speak it. What if you married a person who spoke only Italian? You may tell your Italian mate regularly, "I love you." Your mate may understand from your vocal tone and body language what you're saying; however, when you say, "*Ti amo*!" your words quickly and powerfully hit the heart's bullseye. Nothing says "I love you" more to a quality-time person than focusing all your attention on him or her. You can offer expensive gifts, service and wash the car, leave little love notes in their lunch, and nuzzle with your mate regularly, but until you stop all the talking and doing and focus your attention on him or her, the love gauge needle will move very little!

A God-Send for Marriages!

I've used this tool for a couple of decades in my pre-marital and marriage coaching as the most practical tool for building love into or back into a marriage. When the couple and I begin discussing the love languages I tell them they will likely very easily identify their own love language, *but* they need to be most concerned about their spouse's love language. Done correctly, you may forget your own language as long as you know your spouse's!

Let's go back and pick up a thread and bring it to this chapter. We began with a statement:

If you do marriage:

- God's way
- with God's help
- you get God's results:
  o A marriage filled with divine purpose,
  o holy passion,
  o and with happiness as a byproduct!

In chapter 5, we described marriage in biblical terms as a reflection of the love of God witnessed in the life and death of Jesus. We offered Jesus' words to would-be followers (Luke 9:23) as the model for married love. To refresh your memory, Jesus said to those who would follow him: "Whoever wants to be my disciple must deny themselves and take up their cross daily and follow me" (New International Version).

Rrom chapter 6, add to Jesus' words Paul's writing to the Ephesian believers (5:21). There Paul exhorted the Ephesian believers to allow their marriages to be radically transformed by the act of *ordering under*, or submitting, to each other out of reverence for Christ. The act of submitting to each other looked like respectful love of the wives for their husbands and like cherishing love of the husbands for their wives.

Put the theme statement together with the invitation by Jesus and the words of Paul and you find exactly why the love languages of Chapman serve as the perfect expression of God's love. First, the love languages require selflessness. To love my bride according to her love language, Quality Time, then I must deny myself a focus on my Physical Touch love language. I prefer to hug her, or touch her, or kiss her, or snuggle with her. She likes that, but not as much as spending time with her. She feels deeply loved when I take time to do something with her, like listening as she decompresses at the end of her day. That's my goal as I write this chapter. Mary Beth will arrive home after three o'clock today but will need to practice piano for a while and put on her concert-going garb to accompany a 7:30 p.m. college choir concert. How will she feel most loved? If prepare dinner by 4:45 p.m. and call her from freshening her makeup to dinner served so we can spend a few precious moments together before she's off again. The act of service allows for the quality time she desires. She will pull up to the table and fill both her stomach and her love-tank. I'm going to make some serious brownie points today!

Think about what I will have done. First, I will have denied myself. I will have stopped writing long enough to prepare dinner that we may eat together. I will have denied my preference for hugging her and holding her hand (hard for her to practice the piano while holding my hand!).

Second, I will have taken up the cross today, meaning that I will have sought with God's direction to serve my wife in order that she will be able to serve God better this evening. By topping off her QT love-tank, she may better focus the use of her God-given musical talent on tonight's concert. She and I believe that while she indeed accompanies two college choirs tonight, she also offers her talents used as a gift back to God. She's definitely a better cook than I, but she willingly accepts my meal preparation so we can enjoy each other's company for a few moments. This loving attention sharpens her physically and emotionally and professionally for tonight's concert.

Finally, the following of Jesus may be seen in the actual meal preparation that enable time together. Following Jesus means walking out the sacrifice—the act of cooking dinner. We hear that "the thought counts", but it counts more as it leads to an action. I've tried telling my wife at Christmas or her birthday, "I thought about buying you a one-carat diamond ring. It's the thought that counts." She was not amused!

Get Out of Jail Free Cards

Throughout the years I have used Chapman's *5 Love Languages* to lead a couple to formulate a list of ten concrete acts. Homework before this session with a couple involved each partner identifying the other's primary and secondary love languages. Once identified and before our discussion, each partner would write a list of ten acts that would communicate the partner's love languages, about sixty percent primary and forty percent secondary. The acts should be doable regularly, so the preparation time and money necessary must allow frequent execution.

Then the couples practiced clear and selfless communication by sharing the list, hearing their partner's feedback, and adjusting or changing the list to meet their partner's wishes. Once both had shared and modified the list, I would ask Dianne, my faithful secretary for 23.5 years, to reduce the list to a wallet-size document, then laminate it. I called it a *Get Out of Jail Free Card*. I encouraged the couple to keep the cards handy and to review them occasionally as a reminder of each other's love languages. I warned them that unless they continued to speak their partner's love dialect, they would likely slip back into their own. If that happened, then less love would be communicated and love-tanks would begin to empty.

I wondered if anyone ever kept or used their *Get Out of Jail Free Cards*. I found out in an unexpected manner. In 2008 my younger daughter, Anna, strongly encouraged me to get on Facebook. I didn't want to. Facebook seemed like one more little time-robber. Thankfully, she would not give up. With her help, I entered Facebook world in the fall of 2008. Hours after establishing my account I received a private message from a young lady, Hailey, who was a close friend to my older daughter, Emily. I had prepared her and her fiancé for marriage then enjoyed the privilege of "tying the knot." I sat amazed that someone from whom I had not heard for nearly a decade and who lived nearly three-hundred miles away would be the first person to communicate with me on Facebook! As I read her greeting, I also felt gratified. Hailey wrote that she and her husband were doing very well and that they still had their love languages cards.

Another unexpected incident assured me of their use. I happened to be visiting recently with a couple whom I had known as pastor from their childhood, watched grow up, grow close and become engaged. They granted me the high honor of preparing them for marriage and performing their wedding ceremony. Now, I sat at their dining table in their new home, celebrating their successes and the impending birth of their first child. As I began to leave they mentioned that they had been going through some of their files and had found the file containing the information they saved from our sessions together. Then she said, "And I want you to know we keep our cards on the refrigerator!"

I strongly suspected for all whom I had shown the *5 Love Languages* and knew from our two decades of experience that any spouse who practiced regularly speaking his/her spouse's love language would benefit from a much closer relationship. These two rather random affirmations confirmed Mary Beth's and my experience.

Indeed, I have personally witnessed how the practice of my spouse's love language positively affects her and how her practice fills my love-tank. Furthermore, I have heard from several other couples who have practiced their spouse's love dialect that it works! That's why I continue to use it and I commend Gary Chapman's materials to you.

Here's Where You Find Them

You can find Gary Chapman's book, the *5 Love Languages* quiz (free!), along with podcasts and several other useful resources at the URL: https://www.5lovelanguages.com/. Chapman offers a wealth of applications for the *5 Love Languages*, including for children, for teens, for men, for military personnel, and for the workplace. He also provides helpful resources for dealing with anger, toxic workplaces, and redeeming fractured relationships, and a Bible study guide to help couples grow closer together.

Guarantee

We all like a guarantee. Let me give you one. If you understand and practice the *5 Love Languages*, I can guarantee you that the fire of passion in your marriage will never die. I don't make that promise to you lightly. In fact, I contacted Gary Chapman to ask him if he agreed with the guarantee I had offered. He replied, "*Yes*, it (speaking a spouse's love language) meets the emotional need for love after the high of being 'in love.'"

Speaking your spouse's love language regularly is doing marriage God's way (denying self, taking up God's purpose, and following through) with God's help (as God's Spirit enables you to "order under" your spouse), and producing a marriage filled with divine purpose and holy passion. The husband becomes self-forgetful so he can fill his wife's love-tank. At the same time, the wife becomes self-forgetful so that she can fill her husband's love-tank. Both have love-filled hearts. That should make them happy, don't you think? It's a thumbnail picture of marriage maximized.

CHAPTER 9:

Repairing the Pothole on the Marriage Road

I f you've been married long, you've hit a pothole on the marriage road. No road crew can lay down a perfect asphalt or concrete road that will endure all use and abuse without developing potholes. Likewise, no two imperfect people can lay down a perfect marriage road that will endure all the years and circumstances without developing an occasional bump in the road.

When you exited the sanctuary or wedding venue, all felt right. You could only imagine a smooth traveling on Happiness Boulevard or Charity Lane. The road ahead appeared smooth and clearly striped, like a new asphalt road. In truth, that new, smooth, clearly striped asphalt road hid some issues. On the marriage road, many of those hidden issues could be described as unconscious assumptions and unexpressed expectations.

Definitions

For the sake of understanding, let's define those unconscious assumptions and unexpressed expectations.

Unconscious Assumption

An assumption will be considered a conclusion reached with incomplete data. An unconscious assumption will define a deeply held, usually early-formed conclusion we reached with incomplete data and that operates in our life without our intentional or conscious knowledge.

Unexpressed Expectation

An expectation amounts to one's anticipation of some predicted, desired, or presumed outcome. And unexpressed expectation anticipates some predicted, desired, or presumed outcome, without either clearly expressing the outcome or consciously realizing that one expects the outcome.

Origin of Unconscious Assumptions

An assumption may be unconscious because it develops in childhood through experience and observation. Rarely are assumptions taught us. Our relational values and attitudes are "caught," not taught. We witness and experience relationships in childhood that leave us with impressions. Because our immature brains and/or emotions leave us ill-equipped to process our impressions, they remain as part of the backdrop of our life and color much of what we do without our knowledge. Those impressions shape our beliefs about how relationships should be. We operate by these assumptions without seeing them.

Our frame of reference for our marriage may be like wearing tinted glasses. If you never take them off, then you come to see the world with that tint and think it natural. If you marry someone without tinted glasses, or glasses tinted differently, then you and your partner think you see the world the same way, but don't!

Recently, in a marriage enrichment retreat I led, a young man, Kurt, shared one such rather harmless semi-conscious assumption that proved false with his bride. At the time of the retreat, Kurt and Mandy had been married for four years and had a son on the way. Four years earlier, we walked together through the marriage preparation process and they allowed me to perform the wedding ceremony.

As the retreat group was discussing the *5 Love Languages*, Kurt identified Mandy's primary and secondary love languages. He then observed that when he first married Mandy he thought all women liked gifts. He assumed that because he had observed it in his childhood. When Mandy scored a zero for "receiving gifts" on the love language quiz, Kurt realized his former assumption would not fill Mandy's love-tank. Kurt's mother loved receiving gifts. Because his mother formed much of what he thought of women, Kurt assumed all women loved receiving gifts. He made the astute observation during the retreat that what may have been true in his home and between his parents would not be true for his marriage.

Origin of Unexpressed Expectations

Unexpressed expectations often build on the foundation of unconscious assumptions. These assumptions frame our perspective on marriage, at least in part. They color our view of what marriage should be, so they naturally project into the future as an anticipated outcome.

Let me give you a personal example. Mary Beth and her sister, Melissa, shared a bedroom until Mary Beth went off to college. Almost every night when both of them went to bed, they talked for thirty to sixty minutes in the dark before going to sleep.

Mary Beth married an only child who went to bed alone and who usually fell asleep soon after his head hit the pillow. I called it the result of a clean conscience! Again, Mary Beth was not amused.

Anyway, Mary Beth assumed she'd continue the late nightly conversationss and expected me to join right in. A pothole in our relationship required filling very soon after we married! She'd talk; I'd go to sleep; she'd be upset, maybe even thinking I was rude or didn't like talking to her; I tried to talk, but I married with the assumption that minus any midnight delight, we'd be going right off to sleep as I had done all of my life.

This pothole required several conversations to repair. When Mary Beth revealed the past history of her bedtime conversations and the very warm feelings engendered by their memories, I realized the source of the problem. We worked it out with a compromise. Most evenings we have a brief conversation about the next day, then we share a prayer time together. That has become our mutual, expressed expectation. Pothole filled!

Marking Off Potholes

At least in Georgia, you can occasionally find a circle painted around a pothole on the interstate. An irregular spray-painted circle marks a place to be patched. GA DOT will close a lane of the interstate, cut a square around the exterior of the painted circle, extract the section, and then refill with new cement. This begs the question, how do you identify the potholes on the marriage road?

You begin by taking notice of the rough patches in your relationship. Where do you find that nagging irritation? Where do you experience that frustration, or the extra stress, or the agitation, or the anger? Name the habit or the recurring act. Identify the thing you miss that you want. Start with that gnawing sense of "that's *not* it!" We often have a hair-trigger on the emotional responses stemming from unconscious assumptions and unexpressed expectations. We find ourselves hot and bothered to a degree that seems on calmer reflection to be out of proportion to the actual event. Perhaps, if not out of proportion to the response deserved, our response pushes us in a direction we truly don't believe. Mary Beth thought I didn't want to listen to her, or worse, that I wasn't interested in what she had to say! She came to that conclusion based on what? On her past experience with Melissa. Once we identified and discussed the matter, she saw the assumption.

In my personal and pastoral/coaching experience, I've noticed that the potholes on the marriage road reveal themselves through quick emotional responses that we find difficult to trace to their root. We may know what we feel but we may find explaining the cause of those responses difficult.

Filling Those Potholes

Once you hit a pothole and realize the possible relational damage, you still need a process to successfully repair it. I suggest a two-part process. The first part is preparation, and the second the repair.

Preparation

The preparation requires an inward dialogue that covers our approach to our spouse and a motivation and attitude checklist:

<u>APPROACH</u>: Consider this an attempt to land your relational plane in stormy weather! The atmosphere changed. Landing smoothly became much harder based on the emotional wind-shear! You need a moment to steady yourself before "going in hot." Two things to remember that will steady your approach:

    1. *Your spouse is a person of goodwill* who would not purposefully hurt you or disrespect you. You love this

person. You may not like this lover at the moment, but you stood before Creator and other creatures to enter a covenant with this person. You committed to "order under" God for the sake of God's best will being done in his/her life. You understood, or understand now, that you are called to deny self, take up God's purpose for your spouse daily – like now – and follow through to the very end!

2. *Remember, cherish or respect!* You promised to respect your husband, or cherish your wife (Eph. 5:21-33). That means more in these difficult moments than when life is sunny and breezy. With these two affirmations and a deep breath, you're ready for repair.

MOTIVATION & ATTITUDE: You believe God put you together, or you are willing now to give this relationship to God. You accept the important role as God's primary instrument for shaping his/her life to reflect Jesus' life. In this moment of difficulty, your motivation and attitude sound like this: "I want to help him/her through this difficult moment." Jesus' invitation to discipleship (Luke 9:23) frames your attitude and motivation.

DENYING SELF: Humility will accomplish more reconciliation than pride. To enter the humble-zone, ask yourself a couple of questions: "Am I ready to listen non-defensively?" and "Am I ready to accept responsibility if I was wrong and apologize?" A positive response to both proves you are denying yourself.

TAKING UP THE CROSS: Now you are ready to take up God's purpose for your spouse. This will not be easy, especially if your spouse continues to share negative, or perhaps hurtful, emotions. This will not be easy–the cross never is easy or light or without sacrifice! Therefore, ask yourself, "Am I ready to wade into these negative emotions so I can help God redeem this situation?" Remember, God the Spirit accompanies you because this is holy ground. Whenever forgiveness hangs in the balance, whenever potential reconciliation rests in the next actions, God's Spirit will be there to enable the humbled, faithful spouse. Count on it, whether or not you sense God's presence.

FOLLOWING HIM: All that remains is to follow through. After humbling yourself, breathing deeply, and prayerfully surrendering any negative emotions you may feel at the moment, you gently approach your mate with an invitation to discuss the issue. After all, you love each other, meaning that you are willing to sacrifice so that God's will may be accomplished in your spouse's life. Practically speaking, this translates into accepting your partner as a person of goodwill. It means you do not believe your partner means you any harm and did not try in this instance to hurt you. Once that preparation has been achieved, you move into the Imago process...

The Imago Communication Process

This process grew out of the angst of a broken relationship. One day in 1975, Harville Hendrix, Ph. D., and professor of Family Therapy in the Perkins School of

Theology, Southern Methodist University, walked into his classroom twenty minutes late because he'd been at the county courthouse finalizing his own divorce. As he tells the story of that day, he hoped all the students would have scattered by the time he arrived and that they didn't know why he had been absent. The students were there and had been discussing their own relationships. Three of the students had already married and divorced, three had never been in a serious relationship, and the remaining six were in troubled relationships. There they sat, discussing their own relationship woes.

That day, one recently divorced student posed a question at the end of class, "Dr. Hendrix, why do we have so much trouble in our relationships?" The professor paused and answered, "I don't have the foggiest notion. That's a great question, and I think I'll spend the rest of my career finding its answer."

Making good on that quest, Hendrix immersed himself into research. It also led him to a new companion, Helen LaKelly Hunt, a counselor and divorcée. Together, Hendrix and Hunt wrote the bestselling book *Getting the Love You Want* and stand at the forefront of a therapeutic model to accomplish exactly that, the Imago Dialogue. Their Imago Intentional Dialogue attempts to teach couples how to connect, specifically how to talk so that the other will listen and how to listen so the other feels heard. They crafted the process to create a safe environment for connection.

Their dialogue process contains three steps: mirroring, validating, and empathizing. The process advances in this order:

Sender and Receiver. The Sender has a grievance; the Receiver listens. The Sender's responsibility involves speaking from his or her experience and only using "I" statements (avoiding defenses-raising "you" statements), and speaking non-judgmentally, meaning without blaming or shaming. Keep in mind the Approach and Motivation/ Attitude necessary to speak without a hard edge on your words!

The Receiver's responsibility may seem simpler, but may prove harder: *listen*. Listening involves much more than registering the intake of words. Listening for understanding involves denying one's own emotional response to the message sent. It involves taking up God's purpose of making your partner everything God desires by sacrificing for reconciliation to occur. It requires following this communication process humbly and faithfully to its intended end, or re-connection.

The Sender invites the receiver into dialogue with something very similar to: "I'd like to have a dialogue. Is this a good time?" This brief, direct request alerts you to the need for some kind of reconciliation. You may have anticipated this conversation, or this may be a surprise. If you, as Receiver, feel too emotional at this moment, or for any reason cannot attend to your spouse with all your heart, then say, "No, I need (X amount of time) to be able to dialogue." You may need to go through the preparatory process and ask God to adjust your Approach and Motivation/Attitude. Taking that time in prayer and preparation will prove worth the time. As soon as you can enter the dialogue with humility and faithfulness, say "yes."

The Sender begins the dialogue by stating the issue in precise and personal terms. The statement may sound like, "I want to discuss how I feel about the way I'm left alone at public functions," or, stated a bit differently, "What bothers me is how uncomfortable and lonely I feel with being left alone at public gatherings." Notice the absence of blame or shame, which would sound like, "What bothers me is how you just walk off and leave me by myself at public functions. You know I hate that!" One draws a person into the conversation by sharing personal pain. Sharp and pointed words sets the recipient on the defensive.

The Sender's message remains brief. The Sender avoids ranting and dumping a truckload of emotion and guilt on one's spouse.

The Receiver listens with ears and eyes and heart. The Receiver does not interrupt externally with words, or internally with thoughts of how you will respond. If you begin to frame your response while your spouse is speaking, you cease to listen! That precious person before you loves you enough to seek reconciliation through intentional dialogue. She or he deserves your full attention for this brief moment.

STEP ONE: Mirroring. Once the Sender completes the message, the Receiver begins the mirroring process with three statements:

- "Let me see if I heard you correctly. You said..." simply reflecting the message back in simple, concise language;
- "Did I hear you completely?" or "Did I get all you said?"
- "Is there any more?"

The Sender does not respond until the Receiver completes the mirroring process. If the Sender does not yet feel completely heard, then he or she sends a clarifying statement back to the Receiver. The Receiver suspends any emotion and focuses again on the Sender's message. The goal is not to be right, it's to be loving. In this dialogue, the most loving act possible by the Receiver is to listen! The Receiver mirrors back the clarifying message in his words and asks if he/she heard completely this time and if there is any more to hear. This mirroring process continues until the Sender agrees that the Receiver understands completely and the Sender has completely communicated all the feel content. The Receiver then moves to Step Two.

STEP TWO: Validation. The Receiver seeks in Step Two to show his/her love by giving value to the Sender's feelings and opinions. Valuing may not mean agreeing, but it does mean taking seriously your spouse's feelings. So, the Receiver offers a grand summary, "Let me summarize your concern and feelings: you happily attend these public events with me because you love me, but when I walk away from you to talk to others you feel lonely in the crowd of persons you do not know." Then the Receiver asks for verification: "Does it feel like I'm getting your concern?" If not, the Sender clarifies. When the Sender answers "yes," the Receiver continues with the validating statement, "What you're saying makes sense to me because I know most of the folks attending and you came to be with me, not by yourself, and because you don't like crowds, especially when you don't know anyone, so you are left by yourself." Finally, the Receiver asks, "Is this accurate?" The Sender either clarifies further, which begins another round of validation, or agrees. Upon agreement, the process moves to Step Three.

STEP THREE: Empathy. The Receiver now empathizes by naming the feelings associated with understanding the issue. The Receiver names the negative emotion felt by the Sender, "You are left feeling neglected and awkward and very uncomfortable." The simple, brief statement contains feeling words. The Receiver does not embellish any more than the Sender. King Solomon spoke about the person who floods others with words, Proverbs 10:19 (English Standard Version): When words are many, transgression is not lacking, but whoever restrains his lips is prudent.

After the empathizing statement, the Receiver asks, "Is that what you're feeling?" Again, the Receiver seeks only to listen so well as to make his/her spouse feel understood so they may reconnect. If the Sender offers more clarification, then the Receiver celebrates the communication, listens further, processes, and restates the empathizing statement and asks for feedback until the Sender is satisfied.

Loving action completes the authentic understanding and empathizing. The Receiver then offers an action, "I'm sorry for leaving you so that you feel neglected, awkward, and uncomfortable, so in the future, I intend to take your hand or your arm when we arrive and not leave you unless I discuss it with you first and remain away only a short time. Do you think that will make you feel better at public functions?"

The Imago Intentional Dialogue goes a step further to encourage the swapping of roles. The Sender would then ask, "Would you like for us to swap roles?" The Receiver may say, "Yes, I'd like to be the Sender so you can understand I sometimes feel torn between you and the necessary work-related conversations that occur at these events." The couple's humble, faithful sharing allow for a full reconnection. Each time a couple exercises their love and respect for a reconciling reconnection, their marriage grows stronger in its connection. The marriage road feels smooth again!

Marriage Under Repair

Don't mistake the potholes for a faulty road, or the unconscious assumptions and unexpressed expectations for a faulty marriage. Accept them as opportunities to grow personally with the surfacing of hidden, long-standing issues, to improve your communication skills, and to reconnect and strengthen your marriage. Repair remains possible for the humble and faithful.

CHAPTER 10:

Supporting Each Other for the Long Haul

Since God considered marriage a life-long relationship, we need to learn how to support one another on this extended journey. God promises to support us in that effort, but we experience that divine support through each other.

We've considered the implications of Jesus' invitation to follow him on the marriage relationship. We have applied to different areas Jesus' clear directions to deny self, take up the cross daily, and follow. We've seen how Paul's rather radical idea of submission fits Jesus' directions for following. Now we consider another couple of areas of relationships that will increase the support built into the relationship.

Four Personality Traits

We saw the importance of knowing each other's personality type but each of us can be measured by four personality traits that significantly shape the marriage relationship. David Olson, developer of the PREPARE/ENRICH Inventory, identified those traits as assertiveness, self-confidence, avoidance, and partner dominance.

The PREPARE/ENRICH Inventory represents rigorous research and synthesis, continued improvement, and repeatedly proves it's scientific trustworthiness through many independent validation studies. The continual improvement and repeated validation of its scientific reliability explain the longevity and wide use of the Inventory. Perhaps you see why I have used it for over two decades with scores and scores of couples. PREPARE/ENRICH remains the best instrument for marriage preparation on the market.

The P/E inventory taught me the importance of these four personality traits. Even though couples I prepare for marriage examine their personality types (Keirsey Temperament Sorter), the couple benefits from understanding the individual measurement of these four traits. The KTS measures their personality preferences, while the P/E inventory measures personality traits.

Traits Named and Defined

Olson identified the four traits as assertiveness, self-confidence, avoidance, and partner dominance. He defined them as following, directly from his training manual, PREPARE/ENRICH Counselor's Manual, Version 2000:

Assertiveness – is a person's ability to express their feelings to their partner and be able to ask for what they would like.

Self Confidence – focuses on how good a person feels about himself/herself and their ability to control things in their life.

Avoidance – is a person's tendency to minimize issues and reluctance to deal with issues directly.

Partner Dominance – focuses on how much a person feels their partner tries to control them and dominate their life.

Personality Trait 'Seesaw'

To picture support in marriage, imagine with me two children playing on a seesaw. Enjoying the seesaw requires that one child support momentarily the other child on the upward arc and at its peak. Then gravity pulls the supported child down and the legs of the supporting child propel him child on an upward arc. Supporting roles reverse, as the child on the downward arc momentarily supports his or her friend.

You have a picture of how these four traits relate. If assertiveness measures high for an individual, it means that avoidance must be low. If avoidance goes up, assertiveness goes down. There's a direct correlation. Do you see it? I saw it! (Ugh! Bad pun!) One can no more assert and avoid at the same time as she or he can simultaneously be up and down on the seesaw. Likewise, a self-confident person lives with high self-esteem and a healthy control of things in her life. On the other hand, partner dominance measures how one feels smothered and stifled by her partner. Again, these feelings stand opposed to each other.

I've noticed too that when someone scores highly on assertiveness she most often possesses a good measure of self-confidence. Being able to ask for what one wants and express one's feelings requires an equal measure of confidence. Because the positive traits are often related, they may both be high or low together.

The same pairing may be observed with avoidance and partner dominance. If someone feels dominated by her partner, and if that continues over a period of time, then she likely begins avoiding communication with her spouse. Why pose a feeling or opinion that will suffer his withering control? Her withdrawal makes sense, doesn't it?

The Support Seesaw in Practice

The significance of the personality traits may appear clearer if applied to the other areas previously covered.

The Support Seesaw and the 5 Love Languages

For example, an assertive and self-confident spouse with Physical Touch as her primary love language could ask, "Would you please hold me? I'm feeling afraid as I face my surgery!" A Physical Touch love language spouse who avoids expressing feelings and who feels dominated by her partner would likely not express her feelings of anxiety for fear of her feelings being rejected and/or "handled" instead of valued.

The confident Quality Time spouse may assert her desire, "Can we sit down and discuss a troubling conversation I had with my supervisor today? I'm worried that my job is in jeopardy." The partner who feels dominated and fears sharing his feelings likely sits alone with his feelings instead of asking for his wife's support in carrying that load.

The self-confident Words of Affirmation spouse facing a huge presentation to the boss and his entire team of colleagues may request assurance, "Do you think I'll do okay on this big presentation? I'm anxious about presenting before the big boss and my team!" Sadly, the fellow who grew up in a home marked by avoidance of feelings and who already feels dominated by his wife refuses the urge to share his anxiety. Neither his parents nor his wife created a safe place at home for personal transparency and vulnerability.

You may apply these traits with the remaining two love languages.

Personality Preferences and Traits

Notice how personality traits affect personality preferences. The assertive feeler may ask her thinker husband, "Hey, you're an excellent problem-solver. Can you talk through this issue I'm facing?" The avoider holds in the issue and the troubled feelings surrounding that issue.

A perceiver with an assertive strength may seek the help of his judging wife, "Wow, this project needs some organizational help. I could use your help. Would you mind?" The partner already feeling controlled soldiers on without asking for help. Why open oneself to more control?

The introverted-feeling wife in need of a replacement automobile may lean on her introverted-thinking husband for the price negotiation, "Please handle the negotiation with the salespersons. I'll support you, but you know I'm not the negotiator!"

Unconscious Assumptions and Unexpressed Expectations on the Seesaw

In an assertive and confident marriage, one spouse rightly assumes his or her spouse desires open and honest communication. Based on this assumption, one spouse may expect that his or her partner will listen and value a message shared. Even in moments of conflict, the couple feels safe to request to enter the Imago Dialogue by requesting a conversation. The positive and safe relationship allows for conflict to be faced openly. Whatever unconscious assumptions surface, or whatever unexpressed expectations come to light, pose a smaller threat to the assertive and confident couple who treat each other as persons of goodwill. The strength and safety of their marriage enable growth through conflict.

Couples who suffer from the tendency to avoid difficult feelings and settings, and the couple with a partner feeling the emotional chokehold of a dominating partner, do not fathom the depths of conflict, no matter how shallow. The negative energy of unresolved conflict may well act as a repelling force, pushing partners away from each other and weakening the forcefield that kept the marriage together.

Seesaw Down

Discouragement. Avoidance anchors the support seesaw to the ground of discouragement. Avoidance closes the door on communication and conflict resolution that assertiveness opens. Avoidance leaves one partner to guess the needs of the other. Such guessing becomes discouraging for both spouses, especially since most of us men can't even take a hint, much less intuit our bride's mind!

Seesaw Empty

Fear and Anger. While avoidance stops the support seesaw's motion, partner dominance often kills a relationship. The human spirit needs some sunlight, oxygen, and a measure of freedom to flourish. Partner dominance smothers the breath out of a relationship and blocks the light of love. Further, the controlling nature of partner dominance constricts the relationship as to rob it of room to grow!

Keep the Seesaw Moving

The give and take of seesawing makes it fun. By its very nature, seesawing requires two cooperating participants. Watch children laughing and gleefully squealing on a seesaw. Each takes a turn supporting the other in the air.

A marriage, as intended by God, requires the same. If only one spouse sits on the support seesaw, support is not possible. That one spouse sits motionless. The fun of marriage comes from each partner taking a turn being under the other and pushing up. Each takes a turn supporting the other in the air. Now, take this as a picture of the best marriage – the one God intended for you two! If you deny self, embrace a selfless purpose, and follow through, if you act humbly and faithfully, then keep the seesaw of support moving and you can support your mate for the long-haul, helping to maximize your marriage.

CHAPTER 11:

The Miracle of Gratitude

How many times have we heard, "Sticks and stones can break my bones, but words will never hurt me"? Personal experience told us – and scientific research tells us – that is false! Words do hurt. Sharp words cut. Angry words wither the spirit. Sarcastic words sour a relationship. Contemptuous words pound down another's esteem.

One statistic stuck with me from a senior-year communications class. Lecturing on group dynamics, the professor related that in groups, like committees, the influence of one negative comment requires four positive comments to overcome. How many times have we seen this in our own relationships? We speak one wayward negative word and we spend hours trying to repair the damage done!

According to 1999 marital communication research by Gottman and Levinson, the effect of one negative comment requires at least five positive comments to overcome. (Gottman & Levenson, *What predicts change in marital interactions over time? A study of alternative methods*) In our closest relationship, a negative word weighs heavier! Again, we know that a sharp word from a loved one cuts deeper than those of a stranger, right?

Much traditional research in marriage focused on the negatives that damage marriages, as the medical community primarily focused on diseases rather than on what keeps the body healthy. Recently, however, a body of research has been growing around the positive effects of gratitude on marriage. Here are a few of the findings:

Our Negative Nature

Research demonstrates that we humans tend to "emphasize the negative processes that can lead to relationship distress." By nature, we look for and respond most easily to negatives. This capacity enabled our ancestors to survive in much more dangerous environments than most of us face today. The fight or flight response occurs very rapidly. According to an on-line Harvard Medical School article, "the wiring is so efficient that the amygdala and hypothalamus start this cascade (of epinephrine and adrenocorticotropic hormones that prepare the body for fight or flight) even before the brain's visual centers have had a chance to fully process what is happening. That's why people are able to jump out of the path of an oncoming car even before they think about what they are doing." (www.health.harvard.edu/staying-healthy/understanding-the-stress-response) So, our Creator hard-wired our brains to instantaneously attack or avoid perceived danger. The brain's so-called *negative bias* serves well in dangerous circumstances, but what about every day, non-threatening circumstances? We apparently exhibit a negative leaning even when we perceive no danger.

Since we generally find what we seek, then we must ask ourselves if we will seek only the negative in what our spouse says or does. Will we approach every action and every conversation only with our instinctual negative bias?

Neuroscience brings us good news on that front. Our brains have the capacity to change!

The Gratitude Effect

Neuroscientists call the brain's ability to change "neuroplasticity." You've heard how a sightless person develops much sharper hearing? That's an example of the brain compensating for the sight loss by "rerouting" and "upgrading," as it were, the brain's connections to the auditory center. And what works for the loss of sensory ability also works to build new habits. Sharon Begley, journalist and writer of several books on the brain, summarized the hopefulness offered by the understanding of neuroplasticity: "The power of neuroplasticity to transform the emotional brain opens up new worlds of possibility. We are not stuck with the brain we were born with but have the capacity to willfully direct which functions will flower and which will wither, which moral capacities emerge and which do not, which emotions flourish and which are stilled." (as quoted in https://rightmindprograms.wordpress.com/2010/03/22/neurons-that-wire-together-fire-together/)

Athletes talk about muscle memory. Actually, the muscles do not change to accommodate some new skill. The brain changes. In two Oxford University studies, healthy adults were given MRIs before and after juggling training. In one study, the after scans detected an increase of the "white matter, the long fibres that connect different parts of the brain together," and in the second study an increase of the grey matter, "made up of the brain cell (neuron) bodies... where information processing in the brain occurs." (https://medium.com/oxford-university/the-amazing-phenomenon-of-muscle-memory-fb1cc4c4726)

Do you see the hope for all of us in the human brain's plasticity? We are not destined to remain negatively biased. We can move our emotional brain to recognize the positive in our circumstances, not just the negative. We still have the hardwiring for dangerous circumstances that will fire so rapidly upon the perception of danger that we will not think, just fight or flee. Yet in non-threatening times we will our brains to seek the positives.

In light of these research findings about our amazing brains, let's consider the miracle of gratitude. At a personal level, we know that gratitude begets gratitude! Not earthshaking, huh? When someone is kind to you, then you feel kindly toward them. Research with married couples strongly confirms the value of an attitude of gratitude. When we receive gratitude or even express gratitude to one person, we will be more likely to feel like expressing gratitude to others. According to Robyn Mitchell in *Thankful Couples: Examining Gratitude and Marital Happiness at the Dyadic Level*, studies considering gratitude expressed between spouses include other significant improvements in relationship revealed:

- Perceived support. Gratitude expressed in marriage tends to cause the spouse receiving the expression of gratitude to feel more supported. How would you like to feel more supported by your spouse? How would your spouse like feeling more supported by you? Here's a simple manner of support – not necessarily easy, but simple. If you're willing to deny self, take up gratitude as part of God's will for your spouse, and follow through, then seeing positive things and expressing gratitude can become second nature!

- Cumulative effect. Spouses who regularly and frequently express and receive gratitude seem better able to weather the storms of life, according to a couple of secular studies. They explain the gratitude effect as an accumulation of good feelings that may be drawn on for strength and encouragement during very difficult times.

Dr. John Gottman stated in his brief video *Relationship Repair that Works* that for years researchers studied repair attempts by senders for clues as to what works. They discovered that very good attempts could fail and poor attempts may work. Gottman and other researchers discovered the reason lay with the receiver, not the sender. According to Gottman, "What made the difference (between successful repair and unsuccessful repair) was really how much emotional money they had in the bank with that person." (https://www.youtube.com/watch? v=SqPvgDYmJnY) Emotional money deposits, especially recent ones, may be anything from being kind or being helpful to being available to one's spouse. Go back to the *5 Love Languages* idea of "filling the love-tank" of your spouse. You may fill his/her love-tank by showing gratitude in any number of ways. For the Words of Affirmation person, you may say words of gratitude, or write a note of gratitude. For the Physical Touch spouse, you may express gratitude by saying, "I really appreciate all you've done lately. Come over here and let me massage your neck!" For the Acts of Service spouse, you connect your gratitude with an act of service, "Hey, dear, I know you hate to take the pooch out in the rain. I'm thankful for all the times you've done it, so let me do it for you this evening." How easy to connect a small gift to your appreciation! You get the picture. Several thank-filled selfless expressions of your spouse's love language will top off his or her love-tank.

You have just made another deposit of emotional money into the love-bank!

- Intimacy. Gratitude expressed in marriage promotes the feeling of intimacy between spouses. Again, gratitude begets gratitude. What if over dinner your spouse seemed elsewhere and you asked, "Honey, you seem to be bothered by something and focused elsewhere. You okay?" After a moment he responds, "Well, I hate to confess it, but I backed into another car in the parking lot at work today. There wasn't much damage, but I know we will have a deductible to pay and possibly a premium increase."

  If your response immediately turned negative (negative bias) and you berated him for another accident and for being careless as usual, or if you turned quickly to pile worries about the finances onto his worry, then you would get a negative reaction in return. If, however, you had been training your mind/brain to seek the positive and took a more positive approach, "Was anyone hurt? Are you okay? Great, I'm just thankful you're okay. We've gotten through tougher times than this together. We'll get through this too!" then you've turned the conversation in a positive direction. Yes, this may be another example among many of his carelessness; however, you've chosen the high relational road, Charity Lane.

- Satisfaction. Marriages in which expressing gratitude is a habit demonstrate a significant increase in marital satisfaction. Mitchell summarized the positive effect of gratitude on marriage with these words: "With the current investigations finding that gratitude significantly relates to higher levels of marital satisfaction, it could be that when gratitude is expressed in the relationship, partners shift their attributions from blaming to a more positive attribution such as taking personal responsibility for one's own actions, accepting the partner's positive efforts, and looking toward a happier future rather than toward a past with negative events."

  We build marriage "wealth" just as we build financial wealth, regular and sacrificial deposits versus irregular and large deposits.

- Conditioning. Gratitude expressed regularly conditions one to see or find more things for which to be grateful. Is your gratitude muscle being strengthened? Do you seek and express gratitude several times daily? Emotionally stormy or wintery days make finding and expressing gratitude much more difficult.

  The Apostle Paul proved to be a master at finding genuine gratitude in all circumstances. Paul exercised his Roman citizen right to "appeal to Caesar" once in his life. Today, this would be an appeal to our Supreme Court, except that the Caesar gave only one of two verdicts, thumb up or thumb down – life or death. During his incarceration, waiting for his day before Caesar, Paul wrote a letter to one of the congregations closest to his heart, the Philippian believers. The short letter contained more joy than any of his other letters in the New Testament, even though he sat chained 24/7 to a Praetorian Guard (Caesar's Palace Guards) in a house he had to rent and eating food he had to purchase while waiting for over a year for Caesar to hear his case! This is what he wrote (Philippians 4:4-8, NIV):

4 Always be full of joy in the Lord. I say it again – rejoice! 5 Let everyone see that you are considerate in all you do. Remember, the Lord is coming soon.

6 Don't worry about anything; instead, pray about everything. Tell God what you need, and thank him for all he has done. 7 Then you will experience God's peace, which exceeds anything we can understand. His peace will guard your hearts and minds as you live in Christ Jesus.

8 And now, dear brothers and sisters, one final thing. Fix your thoughts on what is true, and honorable, and right, and pure, and lovely, and admirable. Think about things that are excellent and worthy of praise.

Paul exercised faith muscle memory almost two thousand years before contemporary science described the neurophysiological process! We can practice Paul's advice and find the real value in all circumstances and express gratitude for it. Practice makes one able, if not perfect. We maximize our relationship as we condition ourselves to seek and find the good in our partner, even in the worst of times.

Building Your "Positive Bias"

Here's a suggestion for reprogramming your brain to see the positive. It comes from Ann Voskamp, New York Times bestselling author of the 2011 book, *One Thousand Gifts: A Dare to Live Fully Right Where You Are*:

"It all began quite spontaneously, unintentionally. One of those things God grows up in the most unexpected places.

"A friend dared me to start counting one thousand things I loved. I took the dare, accepted the challenge, kept track of one thousand graces – on a quiet, unassuming blog. Before I knew it, thankfulness to God began to fully change me.

"What I actually found – startling! – was more daily wonder and surprising beauty than I ever expected. And in a few short years, this daily hunt for God's grace, His glory, had ushered me into a fuller life. A life of joy!... it's not overstatement to say that giving Him thanks has made me – and innumerable others – overcomers."

I commend this transforming exercise to you. Take the challenge of finding at least two "graces" daily, one general and one specifically related to your spouse. Do this for sixty-six days. Why sixty-six days? Because recent scientific research indicates that building a new habit requires an average of sixty-six days. (https://psychcentral.com/blog/need-to-form-a-new-habit-66-days/)

To get started, I recommend Ann Voskamp's simple suggestions. She recommends three things. I break out the fourth from number two:

1. Pray for God the Spirit to open your eyes to the wonder around you. God has more for you in this life than you realize!
2. Receive the grace-gifts God plants along your path each day. Observe each gift for at least twenty seconds so the observation has time to stick. Don't pass by the beauty.
3. Praise God for a world more wonderful than you realized. Cultivate a grateful heart and witness the transformation of your life.
4. Record the gifts observed. You may not be a journaler. Just carry a pocket-sized notebook and pen. Jot down a date, place, and a word or two to jog your memory. I have journaled often since 1985. Looking back over those journals gives perspective over time so I see how God has worked. It's like dusting my past with faith and discovering God's fingerprints where I thought I stood alone!

Remember, with each day's discipline you cultivate new neural pathways that build a new and positive habit.

The Reward

Let's make this chapter's connection with God's goal for your marriage. What is your purpose under God as a spouse? Again, to be God's chosen tool to make your spouse holy. God put you two together on purpose for a purpose. God wants your spouse to experience divine love, which is unconditional. Jesus called would-be followers to deny self, take up the cross daily, and follow him. Translated into your marriage, God calls both of you to forget about yourself, take up God's purpose for your spouse, and follow through. Paul taught that in practice this amounted to voluntarily ordering under your spouse, submitting to your spouse as you would to God in Jesus Christ. It's submitting to God in Jesus Christ as the Christ did to His Father.

Gratitude provides a very positive and selflessly sacrificial manner to get under and lift up your spouse. What better way than to keep your spouse feeling positive and ready to serve than to express regular gratitude!

- Helps your spouse feel more supported
- Helps your spouse appreciate you more
- Leads him to be open to acknowledging more of God at work in and around him, thereby making your husband more sensitive to God
- Puts your beloved in a better humor and more likely to desire more often to serve others and express gratitude to them

You want to take your marriage to the next level? Try gratitude. I'm confident your spouse will be grateful to experience your attitude of gratitude. Therein is the reciprocating miracle of gratitude in marriage.

CHAPTER 12:

Time for Some Serious FUN!

How much fun have you and your companion enjoyed in the past month? If you're young and you've passed the honeymoon phase of marriage but don't yet have children, then you may have evenings out to dinner and a movie, or long strolls hand-in-hand. If you have children in the home, two jobs, PTO, church, children's events, a mortgage, car payments, parents to visit whenever possible, and more, then fun together as a couple may be a distant memory!

Here's the truth Mary Beth and I learned several months after our younger daughter's birth. We began to notice that our older daughter looked pale. She had fair skin, blonde hair, and blue eyes, but she looked paler than usual. Then we realized that her eyelashes and eyebrows were missing! Fear of some dread disease soon turned to concern for her six-year-old emotional state when I found lots of her hair in the rear car seat floorboard.

Being the counselor-want-to-be, I immediately recommended finding a counselor who understood play therapy. We found one in Savannah, Georgia, fifty-five miles east of our rural town. The counselor met with us about three times. He spent fifteen to twenty minutes with our daughter and an hour with us each session.

The last session he returns from talking to Emily with this, "I have some good news and some bad news. The good news is that there is nothing wrong with your daughter!"

We waited for the shoe to drop as we asked, "Then, what's the bad news?"

"Well, your daughter is reflecting in her behavior the stress level in the home!" Then the counselor spoke these wise words, "The greatest gift you can give your children is a great relationship with each other! Let's talk about how you handle stress."

While we thought we had a good relationship, we hadn't realized the added stress in our home. Then we surveyed the last two-and-a-half months: Mary Beth's seven-weeks of complete bedrest, my having to add extra parental duties during that time while keeping up my duties as pastor, Mary Beth's recovery from a C-section and a newborn's needs.

We needed to de-stress! We needed to have fun again. Mary Beth and I had to relearn how to have fun. We had lost our childlikeness and had to find it again. The relearning process took time. A few older friends and a couple of teenaged girls provided childcare for us to have that fun.

At first, we felt a bit guilty leaving our small children. Eventually, we understood the value of building this time into our family life. The author of the Old Testament book of Ecclesiastes wrote: "Relish life with the spouse you love; Each and every day of your precarious life. Each day is God's gift" (Ecclesiastes 9:9, The Message Bible).

The advice we received helped to strengthen our relationship. It helped to settle our older daughter's emotions. It helped us to show them a pattern they could carry into their marriages. They learned well that lesson because we now keep our grandchildren for their parents to have an occasional night out. Win/win!

Serious Study about Fun Time

Plato wrote, "You can discover more about a person in an hour of play than in a year of conversation." Therefore, the place of fun in marriage attracts serious attention! For example, the manner one wins or loses a board game or a ball game may reveal something about the way one wins or loses in business or in relationships. The ability to take oneself less seriously gives breath to a harried couple.

Researchers find that playfulness in marriage infuses the relationship with positive emotions and creates a greater sense of marital satisfaction, closeness, and intimacy (Aune and Wong, 2002). Look at the impressive list of positives for the playful couple included in Brower's on-line article, *Have Fun! The Importance of Play in Couple Relationships*:

- Adult playfulness "increases bonding, communication, conflict resolution, and relationship satisfaction" (Baxter, 1992; Betcher, 1977; Kopecky, 1996; Vanderbleek, 2005)
- engenders spontaneity and promotes intimacy (Baxter, 1992; Lauer & Lauer, 2002)
- increases relationship satisfaction and meets the challenges growing out of differences and to weather the storms of life together (Aune & Wong, 2002; Betcher, 1977; Lauer & Lauer, 2002)
- couple fun proves to be the most important factor in the sense of friendship and commitment, and "the greatest influence on overall marital satisfaction" (Markman, et al., 2004)

Let's add one more very practical research conclusion about fun. This one comes from Dr. Arthur Aron, who teaches at the State University of New York, Stony Brook. Aron's contribution to the subject of marital fun comes from the results of one of his earlier studies. Aron recruited fifty-three middle-aged couples. The researchers first measured the couples' relationship quality using standard tests. The couples were then randomly divided into three groups and given different tasks.

Group one received instructions to spend ninety minutes a week in pleasant, familiar activities, like dining out or going to a movie. Group two was instructed to spend ninety minutes a week doing some different and exciting activity that appealed to both husband and wife, for example attending concerts, dancing, skiing, or hiking. The third group received no particular assigned activity.

Ten weeks later, the couples took tests again to gauge the quality of their relationships. The group who engaged in the novel/exciting activities showed a significantly greater increase in marital satisfaction over the pleasant/familiar date night group. Pleasant and familiar prove better than nothing but novel and exciting give you more bang for your fun-buck (Parker-Pope, Tara, *Reinventing Date Night for Long-Married Couples*)!

Armed with these findings to encourage a fun-loving, playful marriage, let's consider how to recapture the fun in your marriage.

The FUNnel

As children, we needed only another willing child or two and we could instantly enter play. No planning or intention was required. Not so much now as adults. Many of us made the shift to adulthood, leaving behind any vestige of playfulness! Yet, here we stand, wanting to maximize our marriage. We may think we want more happiness, but happiness is a consequential condition. It occurs as a consequence of some other decision or action or goal achieved. Seeking happiness as a goal may be compared to trying to nail Jell-O to a tree: try as hard as you can but it continues to fall apart and slip away.

May I interject again that happiness is like the sprinkles on the icing of the holy marriage cake? They look beautiful. Others may see them first, but they do nothing to change the taste of the cake, which will taste just as sweet without them.

Fun in your marriage serves to strengthen the relationship, draw you closer, and build intimacy. When these goals are achieved your marriage will be more of what God intended. You will experience God's unconditional love through your mate. You will understand better both the purpose in your marriage and the purpose through your marriage as you share with others. As you move in this direction, I believe you'll wake one day to find that you are happy too!

Here's a suggestion for recapturing playfulness and fun. I call it the FUNnel. It involves discovery, selfless sacrifice, planning, budgeting, and execution of the plan.

Begin by a list of ten things for each of the following:

1. Things you LOVE to do
2. Things you LIKE to do
3. Things you HAVE NOT DONE but would like to try
4. Things that make you UNCOMFORTABLE
5. Things you WOULD NOT DO

Take one list at a time, starting with List 1, *Things you LOVE to do*. Share. Notice any direct overlapping of the lists. These activities provide a potentially immediate fun list. You have to consider budget and calendar. Yes, budgeting and calendaring may seem like spontaneity killers but with children, jobs, bills, etc. planning becomes necessary. Turn the "why do we have to plan" into "wow, we get to plan our next outing!" You'll be surprised how choosing to a positive outlook changes your attitude.

Notice also the similarities within your list of LOVE-to-do's. How can you tweak or stretch or combine those similar items into another activity or two? Add it/them to your fun list and begin planning.

Now, look at your partner's list. What LOVE-to-do on your mate's list that didn't make your list are you willing to do because your mate loves it? You see what I'm asking, don't you? Your purpose under God is to order under your mate by denying yourself (not only enjoying the shared LOVE to do's but including something specifically your spouse LOVES to do that you don't), taking up the cross daily (in this exercise it means sacrificing for your spouse so that he/she may have some fun – like watching an important football game with Hubby, or a day shopping with your Wifey), and following (through to the execution in a humble, faithful, positive attitude). The ideas of humble self-sacrifice on behalf of your mate and fun don't on the surface seem compatible. Instead, they may represent a high expression of marriage done God's way, and when done with God's help, these activities yield God's results: a marriage reflecting divine purpose, holy passion for each other, and happiness for good measure!

With this in mind, take each list in turn and find the overlaps, similarities you two can work with, and a gift to each other. The third and fourth lists may contain some acceptable novel/exciting possibilities that will supercharge your fun experience. Be willing to stretch some. Also, be aware of your beloved's CAN'T do it/WON'T do it list. Even if something you love to do appears on your mates CAN'T/WON'T list, be gentle and respectful. The Golden Rule applies here.

You should have a list with a number of possibilities. Time to pour them into a FUNnel. Your goal will be to have some measure of fun daily. Yes, daily! Sound tiring? Fun should be energizing. Choose something that you intend to do every day to bring a bit of fresh air into the relationship. Tell each other a joke. Tickle each other. Give a foot rub. Listen to a favorite playlist. Dance together. We're talking about ten to twenty minutes. This should require very little planning or money or time but it punctuates the day with something fun or playful. Okay, so you don't make it every day. Fine. If you aim at it daily and miss it a couple of times each week, how much more fun will you have in your relationship?

Next, plan something weekly. Dining out. A movie. Rock-climbing at the gym. Serving in the local food pantry. Planning a mystery drive for your spouse. A picnic at a nearby state park. This will take some planning and budgeting. This fun time will require more time. The goal is weekly time, if schedule and finances allow.

With daily and weekly plans, now consider something monthly and quarterly. Some of these may be the novel/exciting variety of activities. Have you tried ziplining? What about trying your hand at golf? Going on a bit of a challenging hike that includes beautiful vistas. Kayaking or canoeing. Symphony concert. Dressing up and going to a play. These novel/exciting activities will be worth all the planning and budgeting. Don't leave them out! Special concerts, symphonies, a play, or an overnight at a bed-and-breakfast deserve and demand months of planning but you may have a memory to share for a lifetime.

Finally, what about an annual event? If you have a vacation with the kids, can you work in a shorter time for yourselves? What about a beach or mountain trip for three or four nights? Many state parks offer reasonable rates in beautiful settings. Do you have a friend who may offer you a reduced rate for their beach condo? You can catch some great last-minute cruise prices. The preparation for this trip may keep you in a low-level of excitement for months as you look at restaurants, consider free and fee'd activities in the area, and talk to friends who have visited that area or once lived there. You can catch seasonal clothing sales for a new outfit or a comfortable pair of shoes for the trip. You can fully or partially plan your trip itinerary. You can watch travel programs or read travel books on the area. Talk it up regularly! Savor the preparation. Milk this annual trip for fun before you leave, on the trip, then in the after-glow.

The FUNnel

FUN MARRIAGE!

Grab paper and pens, calendar, and laptop. The time has arrived to recapture that spark – the fun – you remember from your courting days! Remember the wisdom of scripture and of our counselor. From the Bible, Ecclesiastes 9:9, "Relish life with the spouse you love; each and every day of your precarious life. Each day is God's gift." From a wise counselor, "The best gift you can give your children is a great relationship with each other!"

You can begin to spread that relish today (Eccl. 9:9) and infused some levity and reduced stress at home. It's time for some fun, isn't it?

CHAPTER 13:

Challenges on Charity Lane

When we first met, you may have been traveling on the broad and winding marriage road, Happiness Boulevard. Like almost all of us, you had been convinced that we marry for love so we can be happy. You know, the fairytale version of marriage – happily ever after.

We met through this book because you and your partner experience happily-for-a-shorter-time-after. The sunshine of happiness shined on you for days or weeks after the wedding. Then the clouds of life crept back into the sunny picture. Jobs. Rent or mortgage. Car payments. School loans. Within a few months, the new wears off the relationship and you begin to acknowledge a few blemishes on the relationship that you ignored before the wedding.

He has some gross habits. She seems clingy. These existed before the wedding, but the light of love blinded you. No longer!

You began to long for that happiness you were promised, if not by your spouse, by TV scripts, movies plots, romance novels, and magazines. You hoped someone could tell you how to reignite that spark and fire up that passion. You wanted to put the happiness genie back into the marriage bottle.

No such wish-granting genie may be found here. In fact, I believe God, not some fairytale genie, created marriage. Furthermore, I firmly believe that God did not create marriage to make you happy! God likes a happy marriage, but He planned much more for your marriage than happiness. God planned for you to realize an eternal purpose in this relationship. God planned to fill you with a divine passion for each other and for Him. God meant for your marriage to shape your life into the being He intended, and God planned to use you and your spouse to accomplish that in each other.

God created the marriage relationship to be permeated with a divine love that finds expression in humility, selfless sacrifice, and faithfulness. God's love transforms marriage from a focus on self and personal happiness to focus on God's will being accomplished in your spouse's life. A life filled with God's purpose may be called a holy life. In the Bible's two primary languages, the word "holy" means to be set apart by and for relationship and cooperation with God. So, a holy marriage belongs to God, who sets the relationship apart for a divine purpose. Here's where happiness fits into a holy marriage: as a couple progresses in God's direction, they are bound to experience happiness as a consequence of realizing divine purpose and love!

Couples experience that divine purpose and love and the attending happiness on Charity Lane. We've done some sightseeing on Charity Lane. As with all sightseeing, you mostly see the best. I hope you beheld enough potential beauty to desire this path. However, let me offer a full disclosure: you will encounter challenges on Charity Lane. Marriage God's way may not be easy, but it's worth it! The direction we humans tend to point marriage, i.e., happiness, cannot yield divine purpose and passion. Happiness Boulevard promises a quality of relationship it cannot produce for the long-haul. God not only promises that marriage done according to the divine plan yields God's results, but God the Spirit also enters every willing marriage to enable the partners to live as a humble, selflessly sacrificial, and faithful partner in relation to God and to the spouse. God's way with God's help yields God's results!

Here's the good news—the God who abides with you strengthens you to meet every challenge encountered on Charity Lane. Let's briefly look at five potential (guaranteed?) challenges you'll meet.

Potholes

We've already identified the unconscious assumptions and unexpressed expectations every partner brings into marriage as the potholes along marriage road. You will hit a pothole every now and then. Let's call them inevitable.

When you encounter a pothole, don't take it as evidence that your marriage road is doomed. You are human, therefore you will act out of some unconscious assumption, or you will relate to your mate with an unexpressed expectation, which may have blossomed unseen from the hidden-to-you assumption.

Remember, take a deep breath, remind your defensive self that your spouse is a person of goodwill, and remember your purpose under God in this relationship. This painful pothole presents an opportunity for you to order under your spouse, deny yourself the natural defensiveness welling up in you, take up God's purpose for your spouse – humble yourself in this moment, seek understanding and reconciliation, and follow through by bravely entering those negative emotions with your spouse.

In the Imago Intentional Dialogue, developed over decades of use and refinement, you also have a dialogue process to lead you through the assumptive or expectant confusion to the solid ground of reconciled understanding. The steps may appear uncomfortable at first. The language may seem unnatural, even wooden. Trust the process! Practice the steps until, like a dance, the once-awkward steps become familiar and second nature.

Potholes lie in your relational future. You now have tools for repairing them. Don't just wish for a smooth path, allow God to repair those potholes through you!

Roadside Distractions

I'm not a prophet, but I see roadside distractions on your journey. Sometimes I think some enemy has deployed Weapons of Mass Distraction against my marriage. Can I get an amen?!

The whirlwind pace of life coupled with its extraordinarily cluttered personal calendar makes for distracted living. We find ourselves barely able to focus on one event before our attention is ripped away to another event. And if you tend to be easily distracted by shiny objects, then you find our world filled with shiny, mostly meaningless objects! Distractions at every turn.

Roadside distractions challenge you to remain intentional and mindful of your relationship. Fun probably first goes AWOL when you become busily distracted. The busyness of life creates what I call *calendar creep*, meaning the urgent things of life begin to push out the more important activities. In distraction, the fun doesn't seem important when facing the incessant barking of the urgent pack of tasks. Fun seems to be expendable, even luxurious, in the face of bills to pay and places to go and things to do and children to taxi and new demands on the job that gobble up extra hours at home. Is it any wonder that distraction over an extended period leaves one feeling distant from the spouse? Is it any surprise that intimacy wanes in the face of protracted distraction? Do we find any mystery in the lessening of marital satisfaction after weeks of attending to everything but our companion?

Our society stacks the deck against marriage. The promotion of wealth and individualism works against the values of a marriage seeking to realize God's purpose and passion. Our society's value on material wealth demands that we expend extraordinary energy to accumulate money and things. Why not sacrifice fun in marriage, since we're told that our marriage will only be happy when we have certain possessions?

In our society, the individual ranks highest. This sounds good until it's carefully considered. Individualism promotes self-interests. Individualism assumes self-centeredness. How can I adopt God's value of selfless sacrifice on behalf of another and hold to individualism? How can I deny myself if one of my highest values focuses on fulfilling my desires? How can I thrive in between these two opposing sets of values?

If I understand the values of our society and if I understand the different set of values pertaining to the God-directed marriage, then I can identify when distractions begin to pull me away from my chosen path. At least I can eventually identify when I have yielded to distractions.

The FUNnel may provide a measure of protection against distraction. Plan a few minutes of daily fun, an evening of weekly fun, a monthly expression of playfulness, a larger dose of fun quarterly, and a gulp of fun annually. Calendar and budget for these weekly-to-annual plans as an expression of your marital values. Sure, life requires some flexibility, but life does not demand that we yield to the distraction of lesser values!

God gave marriage to us so that we may experience in the two-become-one the unconditional love and abiding presence of the Three-in-one. Distraction hampers God's intention. Keeping the fun in marriage helps couples to take their marriage seriously – seriously enough to maintain the fun in the face of life's urgencies. Maintaining fun in marriage provides an orbit around God's purpose that protects a marriage from the gravitational pull of society's values.

Fun sounds frivolous to the mind steeped in society's values. I strongly encourage you to play together regularly. As you experience God's intended benefits to your marriage, you will become convinced of fun's value, as an exercise of self-denial and for your spouse as an experience of your selfless sacrifice for his/her sake under God. Yield to the importance of fun, not the urgent distractions along Charity Lane.

Empty Tank

Loving selflessly requires discipline over time. Psychologists who study the mastery of any skill say that one develops mastery by doing the right thing (the skill) the right way for a long time, maybe up to 10,000 times or 10,000 hours of practice (Goldman, Daniel, _Perfect Practice Makes Perfect_).

Chances are excellent that all of us who intend to speak our partner's love language will forget our selfless giving of love and revert to our self-centered seeking of love before we've perfectly practiced it 10,000 times! When we do, our mate's love-tank will soon be emptied.

What to do? A disciplined, daily focus on our spouse unlocks the door for success. We must build into our mindset the practice of thinking how today we will express our partner's love language. Will we need to write love notes, will we need to pick up his or her favorite pack of chewing gum, will we need to plan a knee-to-knee, uninterrupted debriefing of her/his day as soon as we arrive home? Most of these expressions of your spouse's love language require little or no money to execute but they do require some mindfulness to plan. That discipline of mindfulness and intention, those few minutes spent daily holding your spouse's love need in your mind, builds a new neural pathway that will develop over time and with good practice. Discipline implies the next challenge on Charity Lane.

"Are We There Yet?"

How many times on a long trip did your children ask ?", over and over from the back seat, "Are we there yet?" And how did we respond? Probably with something like, "Be patient! The long trip will be worth it!"

We adults also tend to be an impatient lot. We live in a microwave world. Good marriages cook at crockpot speed!

We may frequently face our own impatience as a great challenge on Charity Lane. I've often thought that our impatience grows out of the facts that we abide in a time/

space continuum that differentiates past from present from future. Our situation on the time/space continuum, the value we place on productivity, and our penchant for instant gratification make the virtue of patience very difficult to attain. May I offer a bit of a different perspective on marriage?

God lives in the eternal now and can see our past, present, and future in a single glance. From the divine perspective, the journey far outweighs the destination. We really never reach the destination of marriage. Just like the car is not the end but the means on a trip, marriage is not an end but a means to a great end. Marriage travels into a specific state – into the state of holiness. Once we begin the Charity Lane journey together with God's presence and aid, we've crossed the border. In this life we never reach the end of this territory. Consequently, God's purpose for marriage measures the strength of the relationship, not the distance or time traveled.

Viewing marriage as a journey to enjoy instead of a destination to be reached allows couples to take the miles as they come. Marriage encountered as journey measures closeness of the relationship. Think for a moment of a memorable date during your courting days. Likely, the time you spent together flew by. You remember sharing the same time but without being aware of the time. Instead of time, you remember the greater sense of closeness achieved on that date. You remember your loved one's wardrobe that day, the fragrance he/she wore, and you still feel a tingle when you remember how she/he looked at you or touched you. In light of that amazing memory, finding significance in the seconds, minutes, and hours of that date seems ludicrous. You remember closing the relational distance, not covering miles and counting minutes.

The Wizard of Oz provides a picture for this journey. Dorothy and each of her three companions identify specific personal needs. They set out for the Emerald City, where they believe the Great Oz will meet those needs. The story shows how each of Dorothy's companions realized his need as he acted selflessly on behalf of each other along the journey. They impatiently traveled toward a destination. They realized growth individually and in relationship to each other because of selfless love, not because of the miles traveled.

Our impatience in marriage likely relates to our focus on doing. If we focus on being – being with and being available to our spouse – we will experience more of those time-defying, memorable moments. The aphorism, "You're a human being, not a human doing," applies to marriage too. Marriage is not a destination reached by two persons after a measured distance or time. Marriage is a journey made by two persons growing ever closer to each other and their Creator. Let's focus on beings being on a journey!

Loss of GPS Signal

My younger daughter and son-in-law recently introduced me to a new map app. I've used another map for years. The difference between the two rests in the ability to offer real-time traffic information, like a car on the shoulder of the road ahead, or police or construction ahead.

The GPS signal on either map app, once engaged, displays only a short leg of the trip, maybe a half-mile. We need not see all of the map to know we're headed in the right direction.

Don't we desire to know if our marriage is headed in the right direction? I trust the information you've read will give you that assurance. A positive marital direction is set by acceptance and appreciation of your spouse's personality differences as potential strengths, knowing and speaking regularly and frequently your lover's love language, building support in your relationship through regular expressions of gratitude, understanding and communicating your assumptions and expectations, respectively, and taking fun seriously.

Somewhere along Charity Lane, you will realize that you lost your GPS signal. You feel like you're driving blind. You wonder if you're headed in the right direction. It will happen. What do you do?

You use your relational compass. What's that? God offers biblical guidance and the Spirit's inspiration to take a measurement of God's purpose in your marriage. Take a reading of where your marriage stands by asking: Are your actions pointing toward humility (self-denial), toward selfless sacrifice (putting God's purpose for your spouse before your own), and faithfulness (following through to the end); are you voluntarily ordering yourself under your spouse by showing him respect/cherishing her out of your respect/love for God in Christ? Positive answers show that you're headed in the right direction. Soon the signal will return to your marital GPS.

Many of the issues covered earlier in this chapter may obscure your direction. You may slip back into a self-centered desire to have your own love-tank filled, or you see your mate's negative qualities instead of being grateful for his/her positive qualities, or you operate repeatedly from unconscious assumption and unexpressed expectations, or you may lose playfulness in your relationship. When these happen, you've lost your marital GPS signal. You're headed in the wrong direction.

When that happens—and it will happen—pause, check your relational compass by checking the several practical areas covered in chapters 5-10, then realign your actions with God's purpose if and where needed (chapter 4), and step on. Your marriage—and mine—remains on course with regular compass course checks and corrections. Actually, only by keeping your marriage in line with God's purpose will all the pointers offered here prove effective.

You may even call the biblical picture of marriage outlined in this book your GPS, your **G**od's **P**urpose **S**upplied. Use these basics of biblical marriage to guide you and align your relationship with God's purpose in marriage. Your GPS, your biblical compass, always points you and your partner down Charity Lane.

Checklist Review

As you greet each day, I encourage the following:

1. **Expect the good**. Treat each other as persons of goodwill. Enter every challenging time affirming that your companion does not mean you harm. If you assume their goodwill toward you, you will not find ill will where none exists!

2. **Check the love-tank**. How can you top off your spouse's love-tank today? Remember the guarantee: if you each frequently and regularly speak the other's love language, passion in your relationship will never die!

3. **Improve communication**. Practice the Imago Intentional Dialogue regularly. Choose some conflict-free matter as practice material. Use the Imago Dialogue outline to mirror, validate, and empathize. With non-charged practice, you will find the process easier to apply to emotionally-charged issues.

4. **Have some fun**. Take your fun seriously! Discuss it. Plan it. Budget it. Execute it. Your marriage will be stronger for it.

5. **Be grateful**. If you adjust your focus to find the daily gifts from God in general and specifically in your spouse, your life will seem brighter all the time and your spouse will feel much more supported by you.

You will not encounter a single challenge on Charity Lane that God will not help you to meet. As you use the tools from this book and lean on God during these challenges, I believe you will find God's way through each challenge. These tools will make your marriage journey joyfully memorable to the end.

CHAPTER 14:

Lovers Traveling Charity Lane!

Thank you for journeying with me this far. I joined you on the journey that began before we met. You started searching for something missing in your marriage. You remembered the early days of marriage—the excitement, the giddy love, the happiness that characterized your courtship and wedding and early days of marriage. Now, though, the thrill is gone! You want it back. You assumed or hoped someone had discovered the secret to a happy marriage. You Googled and queried friends and searched the bookstores.

Something about this book gave you pause. Maybe the title or the cover? Was it a recommendation from a friend? However you respond, I believe Divine destiny lay behind your pausing here. I believe God wants you to have all the good gifts He intended when creating marriage. The door to your searching mind stood ajar enough that God could insert a thought or desire or impression. You responded by stopping the search long enough to look in this direction.

The brief glance turned into a fixed look. The few seconds yielded to a few minutes of investigation. Was it a novel idea or a glimpse of hope? Then something captured your imagination enough to transform your fixed look into focused attention. You decided to look deeper. You wondered if this novel approach may unearth some happiness secret.

The fact that you've walked with me this far suggests you found something helpful and useful. From chapter 1 I have been pointing you in a new direction.

New Direction

You have seen here a new direction for marriage. New thinking about marriage sets a new direction. These new-to-you thoughts may have included:

- Marriage originated with God, not with us humans.
- God intended marriage to be a two-become-one relationship that expressed God's Three-in-one unity.
- God intended marriage to involve the human couple in Divine purpose.
- Jesus revealed Divine purpose as a life of denying self (humility), taking up the cross daily (accepting

daily God's invitation to be rescued and to rescue others), and following (walking out that purpose to the end).

- Paul translated that Divine purpose into marriage terms when he wrote that we spouses are to order under each other, women by respecting their husbands as an act of worship, and husbands by cherishing their wives in self-sacrifice as Jesus cherished his Bride, the Church.

You realized that God meant for marriage to travel a narrower, straighter path, Charity Lane. On Charity Lane each spouse submits to the other spouse in humility in order daily to accept God's purpose for her/his spouse and to be God's instrument to express Divine (unconditional) love until the end. On Charity Lane each companion becomes God's primary instrument of love to shape her/ his companion into God's masterpiece, reflecting God's image to the world and thereby drawing others to Him.

New Possibilities

Charity Lane offers to break the insanity cycle: doing the same thing over and over and expecting different results. If Happiness Boulevard fulfilled its promises, then fifty percent of those married in the United States would not be divorcing. Yet, most of those who divorce remarry and divorce at a rate of more than sixty percent. Many twice-divorced persons will marry a third time. Statistically, they have a thirty-percent or less chance of remaining married. These statistics on marriage do not count the greater number of folks pairing up and breaking up numerous times outside of marriage! Doesn't this fit the definition of insanity?

Instead, here you learn that if you do marriage God's way and with God's help, you receive God's results—a marriage filled with Divine purpose and Divine love and characterized by abiding happiness as the byproduct. Yes, God wants you to be happy; however, the happiness experienced in marriage comes as a consequence of doing marriage God's way with God's help. God desires to set the couple apart for a relationship with Him and with each other, which is the definition of a holy marriage. As we experience God's purpose and God's love in marriage, happiness grows as a consequence.

The happiness of Charity Lane holy marriage proves to last longer than in Happiness Boulevard marriages. Why? Because the decisions leading to a humble, selflessly sacrificial relationship generate a greater feeling of being valued, supported, and satisfied in marriage. These feelings encourage the reciprocal actions toward the one who gives them and toward others. We not only respond to our spouse's love toward us, but we desire to share that love with others!

Here's the new possibility: decisions (volitions) to humbly, self-sacrificially submit to each other foster feelings (emotions) like happiness and generate the desire to bless others. We feel loved by God through our spouse in holy marriage. We desire to respond to our spouse lovingly. So satisfied are we in this holy marriage that we desire to bless those outside our marriage. In this desire, we begin to reflect God's unity in our marriage and reflect God's desire to rescue others from spiritual insanity. That's Divine purpose or next level marriage!

New Tools

I've offered several tools to help you practically express Divine love. The new tools for your Charity Lane tool chest include:

- *Kiersey Temperament Sorter* (KTS). This abbreviated form of the Myers-Briggs Type Indicator helps you understand your partner's personality and your own. You can see the differences in a non-judgmental manner through the brief test. You can compare and contrast your personalities. The differences may then be viewed as a God-given natural expression of God's creative genius and appreciated. If understood and appreciated, then the differences may strengthen the relationship. Of course, the KTS assumes a basically functional personality.

- *Five Love Languages*. Gary Chapman brilliantly and practically helps us understand the five basic ways we creatures give and receive love. Armed with that knowledge, we may then deny ourselves (focus on our love language), take up our spouses love language(s) daily, and follow through to the end of life "filling our spouse's love-tank." By humbling ourselves and expressing submission by speaking daily his/her love language, God allows our spouse to experience Divine, or unconditional, love.

- *Deeper Communication*. The best marriages will hit potholes on Charity Lane. We all bring unconscious assumptions and unexpressed expectations into our marriages. Eventually, those assumptions and expectations will create a relational bump in the marriage road. However, with the Imago Intentional Dialogue, a couple can repair the relationship – unearth the assumptions and name the expectations. The conflict can be resolved before the marriage vehicle suffers misalignment by repeatedly traveling over these potholes.

- *P.R.E.P.A.R.E.* The PREPARE Inventory identifies strengths and weaknesses in ten critical areas of marriage. By using this tool at the beginning, a couple can set flags at the relational "landmines" to prevent accidental injury. They may then set about disarming and removing them. The couple wishing to use the PREPARE inventory will need to find an approved facilitator. The prepare-enrich.com website offers to connect you to one of the thousands of facilitators available.

- *Gratitude*. Our marriage relationship may undergo a radical improvement if we adopt the habit of seeking daily to find something about our spouse for which we are grateful. Partners who feel regularly appreciated feel more supported and more satisfied in marriage. They also reciprocate the gratitude and they look for others to bless with appreciation.

- *Serious Fun*. The FUNnel exercise encourages small, daily deliveries of fun and creates a calendar of fun activities. Fun taken seriously keeps life operating from a positive perspective, adds buoyancy to a relationship, and prevents it from sinking under the weight of daily urgencies and anxieties.

Need a Guide?

You want your *marriage maximized*. Now, where do you go from here? You see a new direction, new possibilities, and new tools. You know that Charity Lane exists. You can take this information and begin to reframe the purpose of your marriage. You can shift your perspective on marriage from seeking happiness to seeking holiness. From "he's always there for me" to "I'm here for him with God's help." You can try out the new tools. With use over time, you may become adept at speaking your spouse's love language, or resolving conflict successfully. Go now and be grateful for each other and have fun together! Affirm and appreciate each other's personality differences. Use those differences to strengthen your marriage.

I pray that you and your spouse realize the best years of your marriage now and ahead, not just at the beginning. I pray that you realize everything God intended and as a consequence, find happiness too. I hope to hear from you how God has helped you transition to Charity Lane. Please go to www.selflesslove and click the "Book Response" button and let me know if and how this book has helped your marriage. Thank you.

Even though you may together make progress down Charity Lane, if you seek quicker, more profound results, I encourage you to contact me. If we seem to be a fit for each other, I would consider coaching you a privilege. God may lead you to include me on your journey.

To contact me, please go to www.selflesslove.net, click the "Contact Bill" button on the website, fill it out and I will contact you as soon as I'm able. We can get to know each other and explore the coaching possibility together.

While on the site, explore the upcoming retreats. I'd love to meet you there!

May your marriage cake taste sweet because its main ingredients are God's purpose and God's passion and may it be covered with the sprinkles of lasting and significant happiness! In other words, may you be led into a *Marriage Maximized* by God's purpose and passion at work between you and your beloved and through you and your beloved. Blessings.

ACKNOWLEDGMENTS

How can I recount all those who influenced and supported the writing of my first book? I will attempt to mention the ones who most frequently or most strongly influenced and supported the effort.

FAMILY: My bride, Mary Beth, encouraged, prayed for, brought soup during, and now celebrates the conclusion of this book. My daughters, Emily and Anna, expressed and shown pride in Dad's effort spurred me to the conclusion. My mother has cheered for me all my life, and her support got me over many of life's humps and through many challenges, like this one. Other family members contributed by encouraging the desire to write or speaking kindly about some of the things I've written. Some are in-laws (thanks, Sue Barnes) and some are "out-laws" (thanks to you, David Vineyard).

FRIENDS: Many friends encouraged me to write. The voice of several helped me when doubts about worthiness filled my head. Among them are Della Lago, Chuck

Eiland, and Dianne King, who at various times coaxed me to write as we served on staff together within Dahlonega Baptist Church. Several congregational members urged me also – for fear of missing a name I'll simply say thank you for the many Facebook messages/responses. My spiritual brother, Tim Buckner, prayed and prompted throughout the process. My spiritual sister, Nisa Sommers, gave encouragement over a year before I began this journey that helped prepare my mind. A colleague, Christy Greenwald, who writes wonderfully and who spent a number of years editing for a religious publisher, steeled my spine as I began this journey. Her support gave me hope that God may actually use my writing to make a difference in another's marriage.

NEW FRIENDS: I must toss bouquets to Angela Lauria, Heather Russell, Cheyenne Giesecke, Ora North, Bethany Davis, (my editor, whom I have yet to meet), and many other "eggs" in the Author Incubator. You inspired, prodded, corrected, encouraged, and most of all guided this fledgling author through the process. The team at The Author Incubator asked me to acknowledge the Morgan James Publishing Team: David Hancock, CEO & Founder; my Author Relations Manager, Gayle West; and special thanks to Jim Howard, Bethany Marshall, and Nickcole Watkins.

"VERTICAL" SUPPORT: Everyone mentioned so far I count as significant horizontal support. My greatest support may be described as vertical. I am a child of God, a brother of Christ, a "temple" of the Holy Spirit. My life and my *life* come from God, Father, Son, and Spirit. Without the support of my Heavenly Father I would have no life, no purpose, no inspiration, and no significant content to offer.

ABOUT THE AUTHOR

Bill Hutcheson knew as a young teen that he would serve. In early college days he dreamt of being a psychiatrist or a clinical counselor. Mid-sophomore year, he began to wrestle with a call to ministry and assumed he would become a Christian counselor. After graduation, he entered seminary to pursue that passion.

Again mid-way through seminary, God caused a ninety degree turn, this time into preparation for the pastorate. Bill graduated with a Master of Divinity in 1980 and moved to South Georgia for his first pastorate. His thirty-eight years of ministry to three congregations were marked by a love of preaching/teaching and an emphasis in helping couples strengthen their marriages.

His initial counseling interests led to the development of an effective and unique process for pre-marriage preparation. Instead of the typical thirty to sixty minutes of preparation from the pastor, Bill worked six to ten hours face-to-face with each couple. The couples also spent a couple of fun hours doing homework. His emphasis on the marriage, not the wedding, translated to equipping each couple with tools for the marriage road less traveled. Those tools were meant to help the couple build and repair the marriage according to God's plan.

As couples shared their experience with others, Bill received more requests for preparation and occasional marriage enrichment retreats.

In retirement, Bill coaches couples, leads retreats for couple groups, and speaks to congregations who desire happiness in marriage and seek to understand and adopt God's intention for marriage.

Bill, his bride of forty plus years, Mary Beth, and Myrtle, their "Chiweenie" (a Chihuahua/dachshund mix) live in the beautiful Appalachian foothills of Dahlonega, Georgia. Their two daughters and sons-in-law have given them three terrific grandchildren.